The Southwest Expedition of Jedediah S. Smith

The Southwest Expedition of Jedediah S. Smith

His Personal Account of the Journey to California 1826-1827

Edited with an Introduction by
George R. Brooks

University of Nebraska Press
Lincoln and London

Copyright © 1977 by the Arthur H. Clark Company
All rights reserved
Manufactured in the United States of America

First Bison Book printing: 1989
Most recent printing indicated by the first digit below:
1   2   3   4   5   6   7   8   9   10

Library of Congress Cataloging-in-Publication Data
Smith, Jedediah Strong, 1799–1831.
The Southwest expedition of Jedediah S. Smith: his personal account of
the journey to California, 1826–1827 / edited with an introduction by
George R. Brooks.
    p. cm.
Reprint. Originally published: Glendale, Calif.: A. H. Clark Co., 1977.
Bibliography: p.
Includes index.
    ISBN 0-8032-9197-3 (alk. paper)
1. Southwest, New—Description and travel. 2. California—Description
and travel—To 1848. 3. Smith, Jedediah Strong, 1799–1831—Jour-
neys—Southwest, New. 4. Smith, Jedediah Strong, 1799–1831—Journeys—California. I. Brooks, George R., 1929–   .
II. Title.
F800.S55 1989
917.904′2—dc20
89-4939 CIP

Reprinted by arrangement with the Arthur H. Clark Company

Dedicated to
the memory of
DALE L. MORGAN

Contents

Maps

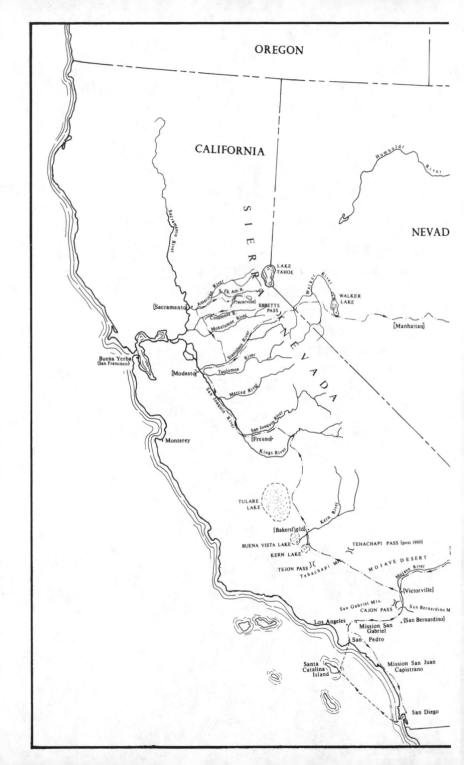

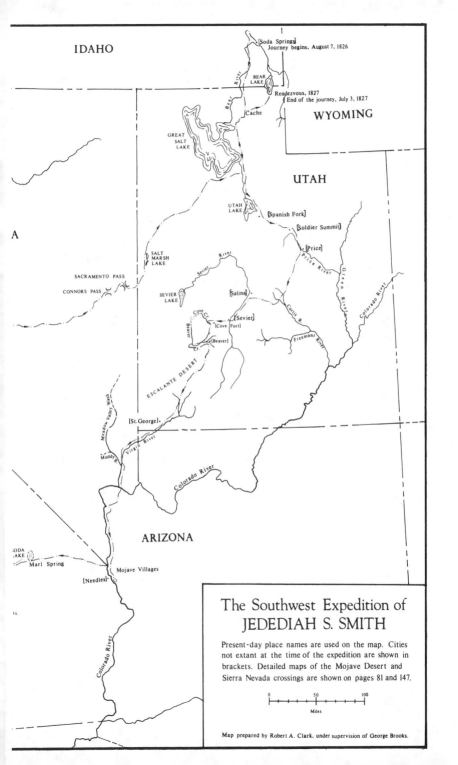

IDAHO

[Soda Springs]
Journey begins, August 7, 1826

BEAR LAKE

Rendezvous, 1827
End of the journey, July 3, 1827

WYOMING

Bear River

[Cache]

GREAT SALT LAKE

UTAH

UTAH LAKE

[Spanish Fork]

[Soldier Summit]

A

SALT MARSH LAKE

[Price]

Price River

Green River

Colorado River

SACRAMENTO PASS

CONNORS PASS

Sevier River

Salt Marsh Lake

SEVIER LAKE

[Salina]

Curtis R.

Cove Cr.

[Sevier]
[Cove Fort]

Freemont River

Beaver Cr.

[Beaver]

ESCALANTE DESERT

Meadow Valley Wash

[St. George]

Virgin River

Muddy R.

Colorado River

ARIZONA

SODA LAKE

Marl Spring

Mojave Villages

[Needles]

Colorado River

The Southwest Expedition of
JEDEDIAH S. SMITH

Present-day place names are used on the map. Cities
not extant at the time of the expedition are shown in
brackets. Detailed maps of the Mojave Desert and
Sierra Nevada crossings are shown on pages 81 and 147.

0   50   100
Miles

Map prepared by Robert A. Clark, under supervision of George Brooks.

Such is a feeble sketch of J. S. Smith, a man whom none could approach without respect, or know without esteem. And though he fell under the spears of the savages, and his body has glutted the prairie wolf, and none can tell where his bones are bleaching, he must not be forgotten. One, at least, who knew his worth, and who had listened with childlike delight to his tales of daring deeds and perilous adventure, can never forget him. But after all, his character as a traveller – as the greatest American traveller – must depend upon his works. When they are published, exactly as he left them, there are thousands in our country, who, thirsting for more knowledge of the "farthest west," will delight to render him all the honor that is justly due him.

Illinois Monthly Magazine, June 1832

Introduction

When the late Dale L. Morgan was in St. Louis in March of 1967 to address the centennial conference of the Missouri Historical Society, he expressed the hope that perhaps the attics and closets of the city might still provide exciting discoveries in the way of fur trade material to add to the Society's already impressive archives on the subject. Some of us who had spent considerable time searching such dusty nooks and corners with discouragingly few positive results tended to receive Dale's words with knowing skepticism and dismiss them as nothing more than the sort of appropriate remarks that visitors are supposed to make on such occasions. We should have realized, however, that the unlimited Morgan optimism and his uncanny perception had sensed something in the air.

About four months later, on a steamy summer afternoon, a friend came to my office with a group of papers he wished to add to a substantial collection which his family had donated to the historical society over the years. Among the things he offered was a simple cardboard box from around the turn of the century with his grandfather's name written upon it. This modest reliquary was opened to reveal two segments of an apparently lengthy manuscript which began with the words: "August 7th 1826 at our rendezvous at a place known as the bend of the Bear River. My Partners Messrs Jackson & Sublette and myself   .   .   ." The remarks brought at once both the excitement of anticipating a discovery of major importance, and the fear that what would follow was not what was indicated. My apprehensions of the latter event, however, were laid to rest by the donor, a student of history himself, who had gone carefully through the text and happily assured me that it was, in fact, a first-person account of Jedediah Strong Smith's southwest expedition of 1826. The story by the first American to make the overland trip to California – an important document relating to one of the great heroes of the early American West – had been reclaimed from oblivion.

How had the donor come by such a treasure? From his grandfather, obviously; the manuscript had rested in its box among the forbear's possessions on the third floor of a substantial St. Louis residence for nearly half a century. But was there any way to extend the provenance back to Jedediah Smith? Our benefactor advanced such a connection which, although it does not explain the transfer of the manuscript from one party to another, seems to establish a chain of circumstances which must be very near the truth. The donor's grandfather, John C. Orrick (1840-1900), was a son-in-law of Beverley Allen (1800-1845), a prominent St. Louis attorney and businessman of his day who was the executor of the estate of General William H. Ashley (1785?-1838). Ashley, in turn, had been the executor of the estate of his own good friend, protégé, and partner in the fur trade, Jedediah Smith. It is most probable – almost certain – that Ashley had possession of the manuscript at some point;[1] perhaps a portion of the papers remained in his estate and for some reason were kept by Allen (Ashley had no children of his own). Although no definite descent for the journal can be established, the facts seem to lie somewhere in the area outlined.

After making a typescript of the journal, I passed on news of the discovery to Dale Morgan, the biographer and great champion of Smith, and in subsequent meetings and correspondence we discussed editing the material. Quite early, he consented to and encouraged the idea that I do this edition, and provided – as only he could – his ideas, inspiration, and enthusiasm. Morgan's untimely death in 1971 ended what had become a joyous and rewarding association for me, and his memory

---

[1] There is also a very clear indication of Ashley's involvement with the manuscript in the following note found at the beginning of the scrapbook discovered by Maurice Sullivan which contains the other portion of the transcript: "——— Ashley I have left the commencement of your business for you to fill up as you are so much better informed of all the circumstances. If it is your choice you can do it as if it had been done by me which from our conversation I suppose you would prefer. The corresponding space I would suggest as being the most appropriate for giving the origin of your business in my words; the chain of narrative would be unbroken."

haunts the pages of this book. Anyone working on
Jedediah Smith today owes almost everything to Dale
Morgan's precise scholarship and stunning biography.[2]

The manuscript is written on unwatermarked pages,
13 by 7¾ inches, lightly lined; it is in two sections of
24 sheets each (in actuality, each segment is twelve
large sheets, 13 by 15½ inches, folded, and sewn in a
very simple fashion) which provide a total of 96 writing surfaces. The paper seems to be similar to that used
for the only other known portion of the Smith transcript, which was discovered and published by Maurice
Sullivan in his important work on Jedediah in 1934,[3]
and which is an immediate continuation of this manuscript. Both Sullivan's and this account are written in
the same hand – that of Samuel Parkman[4] – and even
a cursory comparison of the style or grammar will

---

[2] Dale L. Morgan, *Jedediah Smith and the Opening of the West* (Indianapolis, 1953).

[3] Maurice Sullivan, *The Travels of Jedediah Smith* (Santa Ana, California,
1934). Sullivan found the manuscript in the possession of a descendant of
Benjamin Paddock Smith, a younger brother of Jedediah.

[4] Samuel Parkman (died 1873) first appears as a member of William Sublette's spring outfit of 1829. He returned to St. Louis in the fall of 1830, and
according to an early sketch, "was engaged during the winter of 1830-31 in
arranging the notes, and making maps of the route through which [Smith]
had traveled" (quoted in Morgan, *Smith*, 433 n.37). Parkman was also the
scribe for and a witness to Smith's will which was signed just prior to the
fateful trip to Santa Fe. The will, incidentally, is dated the "thirty first day of
April," an impossibility which has escaped notice until now and which creates
a degree of apprehension about the accuracy of facts and figures in the
transcript.

quickly indicate that the two were once part of a running narrative.

There has never been any question of the fact that the transcript was intended for eventual publication. The eulogy to Smith which appeared in 1832 mentions that "It will certainly be gratifying to our literary men, as well as those engaged in the fur trade, to know that Smith took notes of all his travels and adventures, and that those notes have been copied, preparatory for the press. There may be some omissions in them for reasons which will probably appear in the book itself."[5] And as late as 1840, an announcement in a St. Louis paper gave news of a proposal:

> For publishing, by subscription, "The Journal and Travels of JEDEDIAH S. SMITH," late of the firm of SMITH, SUBLETTE AND JACKSON. This work will take in the travels and adventures of Mr. Smith in the *Rocky Mts., Oregon Territory,* and in *California* for a period of nine years, to which will be attached a map of the Oregon Territory, including all the territory, of the United States west of the Mississippi. To be compiled from the original notes of the traveler; by ALPHONZO

[5] From "Captain Jedediah Strong Smith. A Eulogy of That Most Romantic and Pious of Mountainmen, First American by Land into California," *Illinois Monthly Mag.,* XXII (June 1832), 393-98. The author is usually given as James Hall (1793-1868), the well-known Western literature figure who was editor of the periodical. Certainly the style is very close to Hall's own, but one cannot completely dispel the idea that Charles Keemle (1800-1865) was also involved. Keemle, from 1829 to 1832 the editor of the weekly St. Louis *Beacon,* had been a clerk with the Missouri Fur Company and shared some of Smith's experiences in the West in 1823.

WETMORE, compiler of the Missouri Gazeteer and editor of the Missouri Saturday News.

To be published at the Saturday News office in St. Louis & delivered to subscribers at $2 a copy.

Subscriptions received at the News office, 149 Main St., St. Louis, Missouri.[6]

There is no indication of why the project failed, whether through a lack of prospective subscribers or Wetmore's abandonment of the literary work, nor is there any hint of who then owned the manuscript. The announcement, however, suggests that the material, in whatever form it existed, was still intact. Since then, Smith's original journals and notes have disappeared, probably lost forever through fire,[7] and only two portions of the transcript, Sullivan's and now this, have been located. Is there more of the transcript? No one knows how extensive it was originally, but one can offer the hope that other sections await the light of day so that more of Jedediah's story may be told through his own words.

What a remarkable story it was; and how even more amazing that it was almost totally ignored for over three quarters of a century. For here is the man who was the first American after the Astorians to penetrate west of the Continental Divide by land (after rediscov-

---

[6] St. Louis *Missouri Saturday News*, May 9, 1840. For a biographical sketch of Wetmore (1793-1849), an early frontier traveler and Missouri literary figure, *see* Kate L. Gregg, "Major Alphonso Wetmore," *Missouri Hist. Rev.*, XXXV, no. 3 (April 1941), 385-93.

[7] Sullivan, *Travels*, foreword (no pagination); Morgan, *Smith*, 9.

ering, for practical purposes, South Pass); the first to make the overland journey to California, transit the Sierra Nevada, and cross the desert of the Great Basin (the tale of this narrative); and the first to go by land from southern California to northern Oregon. Perhaps Smith's own modesty, combined with his early death and the absence of any posthumous literary recognition, contributed to his being forgotten by the American public. Even within a year of his death, the editor of the *Illinois Monthly Magazine* noted that: "With not a little concern and surprise, it has been ascertained that the death and character of our distinguished countryman, J. S. Smith, have been entirely unnoticed [in St. Louis]."[8] Harrison C. Dale first "rediscovered" the significant role Jedediah had played in the opening of the American West in his book on Smith and Ashley in 1918.[9] John G. Neihardt's story in the 1920s, Maurice Sullivan's work in the 1930s, and Dale Morgan's nearly definitive biography in 1953 have now firmly established a proper perspective from which to view Smith's accomplishments. With these books, and a fine condensed biography by Harvey L. Carter which was published in 1971,[10] there is no need for any compre-

---

[8] From the Eulogy in the *Illinois Monthly Mag.*, 393.

[9] Harrison C. Dale, *The Ashley-Smith Explorations and the Discovery of a Central Route to the Pacific, 1822-1829* (Cleveland, 1918; and Glendale, Calif., 1941).

[10] Harvey L. Carter, "Jedediah Smith," *The Mountain Men and the Fur Trade of the Far West*, VIII (Glendale, Calif., 1971), 331-48.

hensive study of Smith's life at this point, however some brief remarks are necessary.

Jedediah Strong Smith, born on January 6, 1799, in Jericho (now Bainbridge), New York, arrived in St. Louis in the spring of 1822, already resolved to make his mark as a hunter in the fur trade. He signed with General William H. Ashley – perhaps in response to Ashley's often-quoted advertisement for "enterprising young men" – and left for the upper Missouri on May 8, 1822.[11] After wintering with Ashley's partner, Andrew Henry, at the mouth of the Yellowstone, Smith was en route to St. Louis when he met Ashley coming upriver just in time to become involved in the devastating attack hurled upon the traders by the Arikaras. It was at this point that Smith emerged as a leader from among the roster of dependable hunters. After distinguishing himself by his courage when pinned down by Indian fire on an exposed sandbar in front of the Arikara village, Smith volunteered to go north to seek reinforcements from Henry, and upon his return to Ashley was made captain of one of two companies of men in the Missouri Legion, a force organized by Colonel Henry Leavenworth to attack and punish the Rees.[12] From then on, there was no question of Jedediah

---

[11] Biographical information from Morgan, *Smith*. The Ashley advertisement appeared in the St. Louis *Missouri Gazette & Public Advertiser* for Feb. 13, 1822.

[12] Details of this episode, and other events relating to Ashley and Smith along with a wealth of source material may be found in Dale L. Morgan, *The West of William H. Ashley* (Denver, 1964).

being apart from and above his companions, and his stature would continue to increase. Almost immediately, he was given command of an independent party of Ashley's men and led them directly west through the Badlands and Black Hills in the fall of 1823 to scout for beaver in the region south of the Yellowstone. The party wintered with the Crows in Wind River Valley and in February 1824, set out south in the direction of the Green River. Their course led them across the Continental Divide, where Smith found and made use of a natural transit which would become known as South Pass, an important geographic landmark in the story of America's westward expansion.[13] Moving on to the north after his summer activities, Jedediah came upon some Iroquois connected with a Hudson's Bay Company party near present Blackfoot, Idaho, and through a set of circumstances arrived at a Company station, Flathead Post, on Clarks Fork of the Columbia. Although the British were suspicious of Smith's motives and less than enthusiastic about his presence in what they considered their private beaver preserve, there was no overt hostility and Smith's group wintered along the Snake River with a Company trapping party led by Peter Skene Ogden. In July 1825, after a spring hunt in the general area, Smith met on Henry's Fork with General Ashley, who had come out from St. Louis with

---

[13] The pass had been used – from west to east – by the returning Astorians in 1812, but was forgotten again. Smith's is the first "effective" discovery in an historical sense.

a caravan of trade goods for the first of the annual fur trade rendezvous. It was here that Smith assumed another role, that of a partner in the trade, for Ashley, because of a variety of reasons, extended the business association to Jedediah. The two partners of Ashley & Smith then returned to St. Louis – Smith after an absence of over three years; but Jedediah left again for the Rockies within the month and got as far as the Pawnees on the Republican River before wintering. Ashley followed Smith west with his rendezvous goods in the early spring.

It was at the rendezvous of 1826, just shortly before this narrative begins, that Ashley announced his decision to retire from the type of active role in the fur trade which would require his presence in the mountains. Smith, as Ashley's partner, was a logical successor, and two other of Ashley's men, David E. Jackson and William L. Sublette,[14] joined him in signing the necessary agreements acquiring Ashley's goods and forming the partnership of Smith, Jackson & Sublette. For the story of Smith's epic adventures from then until the next rendezvous in the summer of 1827, we are now fortunate to have his own account.[15]

---

[14] Little is known of the early fur trade activity of Jackson, who is remembered by us today for his discovery of Jackson Hole; his career in the southwest after 1830 is better documented. For a fine biography of Sublette, *see* John E. Sunder, *Bill Sublette, Mountain Man* (Norman, Oklahoma, 1959).

[15] To conclude this rather journalistic account of Smith's life – others have done it so much better – a very brief outline follows. Smith went back to California in 1827 by nearly the same route as previously, but in a shorter time,

Over the years, as students sought to reconstruct Smith's journey to California, a number of questions arose which produced some rather lively differences of opinion. Some of these may now be laid to rest forever and will be mentioned at appropriate points in the text. Other problems, however, remain unsolved; and, perhaps as it should be, this account by Smith produces some difficulties of its own.

An important part of any travel journal is the route itself, and in the case of this expedition, a large portion of the trail has been known, or at least speculated upon, because of Jedediah's comments when he retraced some of his path in 1827. The manuscript at hand now confirms almost entirely what Dale Morgan had laid out

---

to meet with the men he had left behind in this narrative. The expedition was a disaster, two tragedies in fact. At the Mohave villages, while attempting to cross the Colorado, Smith's party was attacked; ten men were killed and the survivors left in uncomfortable circumstances. After joining the Rogers party and continuing on up through northern California to Oregon, Smith's men were set upon by Umpqua Indians on July 14, 1828, and nearly obliterated; only Smith and three others escaped to struggle to the Hudson's Bay Company post on the Columbia, Fort Vancouver. Jedediah remained at the fort until the spring of 1829 when he left to rejoin his partners. During 1829 he hunted in Blackfoot country, along the Powder River, the Yellowstone, the Musselshell, and the Judith; something seemed to have gone out of the business however – the beaver for one thing weren't as plentiful – and at the summer rendezvous of 1830 the three partners sold out to what was to become the Rocky Mountain Fur Company. Smith returned to St. Louis where he spent the winter of 1830-31 (during which time this transcript was written) planning a trading outfit to Santa Fe. Jedediah departed St. Louis on April 10, 1831. On May 27, on the dry flat "water scrape" of the Santa Fe Trail, Smith left the party to search for the desperately-needed liquid. Alone, he came upon a Comanche hunting party; it was all over very quickly.

for Smith's route, the most noticeable exception being the swing into the mountains east from Utah Lake. This was suggested on some maps related to Smith's missing original, but no account of the detour previously existed. Jedediah's journal also proves that Francis Farquhar was correct in projecting Ebbetts Pass as the point for the historic transit of the Sierra Nevada; on the other hand, it stills forever some of C. Hart Merriam's less fortunate conjectures.

Ideally, one should also offer a chronological sequence to go hand-in-hand with the route, but in several instances here that is impossible. Probably Smith's original field journal was kept in diary form, for many segments of this text are treated in that way. However, we are dealing with a transcript, after all, and Samuel Parkman handles the story as a continuing narrative which in some cases confounds all efforts to tie definite episodes with calendar dates. Even the account kept by Smith's clerk, and known here as the Harrison Rogers daybook I, which offers specific dates at certain points, is not all the help in collating the texts that it might seem at first.[16] Where possible, every effort has been made to establish dates for certain sections of the route, but some of the time schedule simply cannot be extracted from the generalities of the transcript.

One aspect of the trip, and a very important one, which has produced an untold amount of speculation, is the question of just what Smith had in mind as his

---

[16] The narrative portions were first published in Dale's book in 1918.

ultimate goal. The idea that, although Jedediah set out in a southwest direction, his true objective was the mouth of the Columbia River (or at least the legendary Buenaventura) has concerned many writers and cannot be set aside casually.

In the present text, Smith states that he set out to the south and southwest not knowing "what that great and unexplored country might contain," but hoping to "find parts of the country as well stocked with Beaver as the waters of the Missouri which was as much as we could reasonably expect." In addition to this obvious commercial motivation, Jedediah adds a personal note of his own by allowing that:

> In taking charge of our S western Expedition I followed the bent on my strong inclination to visit this unexplored country and unfold those hidden resources of wealth and bring to light those wonders which I readily imagined a country so extensive might contain. . . I wa[nted] to be the first to view a country on which the eyes of a white man had never gazed and to follow the course of rivers that run through a new land.

Smith's natural inclinations as an explorer and investigative traveler are admirably demonstrated in this text through his descriptions of the landscape, his interest in natural history, and his comprehensive reports on the Indians he encountered. Elsewhere his maps reveal a geographical concern which goes far beyond that of the average tourist.[17] So these then seem to be the rea-

---

[17] A full discussion of Jedediah's influence on maps of the West may be found in Dale L. Morgan and Carl I. Wheat, *Jedediah Smith and his Maps of the American West* (San Francisco, 1954).

sons for the trip: the search for beaver on the one hand, and an investigation of a new territory on the other. Not one word about the Pacific Northwest, although with the Oregon question still an open issue at the time the manuscript was written, it might not be expedient to mention it. After all, had not Alexander Ross taken a wary view of Smith and his small party as potential spies when Jedediah showed up at Flathead Post in 1824? The rewards of the fur trade along the watershed of the Columbia were too great to risk idle words, and Jedediah would be intelligent enough to realize the fact. But perhaps this is too much conjecture.

After three months on the trail, when Smith was at the Mohave villages along the Colorado, he seems to verify his earlier remarks. Learning that the Spanish settlements in California were but ten days away, he considers his situation and then decides to move in that direction:

> Believing it impossible to return to the deposit at this season and in my present situation I determined to prepare myself as well as possible and push forward to California where I supposed I might procure such supplies as would enable me to move on north. In that direction I expected to find beaver and in all probability some considerable river heading up in the vicinity of the Great Salt Lake. By this route I could return to the deposit.

At this point Jedediah indicates that he apparently changed his mind, and instead of returning to the northeast, decided that various necessities compelled him to make a great circuit up through Spanish California before heading east. There is nothing to suggest that such a course had been his original intention; even the reference to the mysterious great river is not all that significant, for the stream had been thought to be out there somewhere, and it would be natural for Smith to assume its existence and seek it out if the opportunity arose.

Those who have inclined toward the theory that Smith really did intend to go to the Columbia have relied heavily, until now, on a letter that Daniel Potts wrote from the rendezvous on July 16, 1826. Apparently anticipating that he would accompany Smith, Potts wrote that he would leave soon "to explore the country lying S.W. of the Great Lake where we shall probably winter. This country have never been visited by any white person – from thence I cannot say, but expect the next letter will be dated mouth of the Columbia River."[18] Was this more than campfire gossip? Once Smith arrived in California, he seems to have had a trip north – possibly to Oregon – clearly in his mind; perhaps he had decided upon it even earlier.

A new dimension is now added to the controversy in the form of a problem posed by this manuscript, namely the inclusion of Marion, an "Umpquah" Indian slave in the roster of the party which departed from Salt Lake. The first inclination – and it may be the best in the end – is to dismiss this information as a slip on Smith's part, or an error by Parkman the transcriber.

---

[18] As quoted in Morgan, *Smith,* 193.

But since Marion is there right in the middle of the list, the implications of his presence must be considered. Unless one has a distorted view of geography, and certainly this wasn't true of Jedediah, one would not bother to take an Umpqua (a native of Oregon) along on a hazardous expedition whose only aim was to search out beaver and explore in the southwest. Marion's presence, if true, suggests that the Columbia was the goal from the beginning, or at least a very carefully considered option. Until now, it has always been assumed that Marion was the Indian boy captured by the (second) Smith party in southern Oregon shortly before the Umpqua massacre;[19] that was all very logical and as it should have been, but now we have to consider the possibility that Marion was around from the start of Smith's first trip to the coast. If, in fact, Marion was along for the whole trip, his existence gives credence to those who theorize that Jedediah intended to go to the Columbia and pursue the beaver in territory already trapped by the Hudson's Bay Company.

The presence of an Umpqua slave in the general vicinity of the Great Salt Lake seems impossible from a realistic viewpoint, although it could theoretically happen if circumstances are stretched far enough. Brit-

[19] The Harrison Rogers daybook II, which does not list Marion in its roster of May 10, 1828, mentions that one of the party "caught a boy about 10 years old and brought him to camp . . ." (Dale, 242, 270). It has always been assumed that the boy (listed elsewhere as a slave, *see* Morgan, *Smith*, 277) and the "Marion (an Indian boy)" listed as a casualty of the Umpqua massacre (*Ibid.*, 341) are the same person.

ish parties had hunted the territory bringing Indians with them, and possibly an Umpqua slave was brought along by one of the caravans; Smith had been at Flathead Post and could have acquired the Indian in the course of events with the idea he might be useful some day. All this seems far fetched, however. Marion appears nowhere else in either Smith's account or in Rogers daybook I (although perhaps as a menial he might not). It is difficult to accept him, and until further evidence comes along he is best set aside, although he adds considerable weight to the Columbia-as-the-goal hypothesis. The answer would lie in knowing whether Jedediah had a chance to read and review the transcript carefully; if he had no objection to Marion, then the Indian must remain. If Smith did not check on Parkman's work, then an error is possible. We shall probably never know.

About one thing, however, there is no question, and that is the remarkable character of Jedediah Smith which earned him the respect of his contemporaries. His leadership asserts itself time after time in this text, not only in directing the course of his party, but in the concern for the welfare of his men. In the heat of the Mojave Desert he goes ahead to search out water and a campsite; in the bitter cold of the Sierra he strikes on twelve miles in advance of his companions to seek a pass, but discovers only disappointment. Jedediah on that mountain height is a symbol not easily forgotten or ignored. His was an instinct for compassionate command as in that moment of desolation he recalls that he was brought back to reality by the "recollection that [his] party were entirely depending on [his] movement."

It was the ability to think contemplatively that gave Smith yet another strength and made him different from other mountain men. Jedediah could reason and meditate, and his introspection often made him aware of his loneliness:

> It was indeed a freezing desolation and one which I thought should keep a man from wandering. I thought of home and all its neglected enjoyments . . . and visions of flowing fields of green and wide spread Prairaes of joyous bustle and of busy life thronged in my mind to make me feel more strongly the utter desolateness of my situation. And is it possible, thought [I] that we are creatures of choice and that we follow fortune through such paths as these.

But follow Smith did. Determination of purpose was another characteristic, and only in the Sierra did he learn "one thing which I did not know before that I must sometime be turned back." Determined and sober, assertive yet modest and quiet, Jedediah traveled through uncharted wilds observing them with the natural intellect of a true explorer. His was an inner superiority which neither the perfidy of man nor the privations of nature could deny, and it is still vibrant in these pages after a century and a half.

For this edition, the manuscript itself has been corrected as little as possible. Errors obvious as those of the transcriber, such as overstrikes and corrections to his text, have been set to right without mention. Punctuation changes have been held to the bare minimum, and additional punctuation inserted only where obviously necessary. Spellings and the capitalization of some words have been left as they were in the original even though in some instances the mistakes are self-evident. The text could have been smoothed out, but in doing so it would have broken the style and rhythm of Smith and Parkman, and something of the first-hand experience would have been lost. The editing concerned itself more with amplifying the text than in correcting it.

To this manuscript, two others have been added. Because it seemed only logical to complete the entire journey back to the 1827 rendezvous, a portion of the journal first published by Maurice Sullivan – covering the period from June 22, 1827, through July 3 – has been attached to the end of the Missouri Historical Society manuscript. The version here printed is taken from a microfilm of the original, and not from the Sullivan edition. For use of that portion of the manuscript, I am most grateful to its present owner, The Jennewein Western Collection, Dakota Wesleyan University, Mitchell, South Dakota, and the collection's librarian, Mrs. Betty Kugel; Mr. Kenneth R. Stewart, curator of the Friends of the Middle Border Pioneer Museum at Mitchell was most helpful in arranging this courtesy.

I have also appended the Harrison Rogers daybook I, as it is the only known account of the trip by another member of Smith's party. This document, in the possession of the Missouri Historical Society, was edited and published, in part, by Harrison Dale in his Ashley-Smith book of 1918. However, although the narrative portion was reproduced in full, some of it was transcribed inaccurately, and nearly all of the account and ledger entries relating to this trip were omitted. And too, there is also good reason to suspect that Smith, who had recovered the Rogers notes after the Umpqua massacre, used them where his own were lacking as the basis for portions of this narrative in this journal.

As a final remark, it should be noted that this edition is based primarily upon amplification through literary sources and maps. Outside of my own general awareness of much of the area through travel, there was no opportunity for me to undertake the field expeditions necessary to verify my suppositions or conclusions. I am most grateful to Mr. Todd I. Berens of Santa Ana, California, and a remarkable group of his students in the Explorer Club of the Walker Junior High School in Santa Ana for their assistance in doing some field work as a courtesy to Dale Morgan and a great help to me. This was only a bare beginning, however, and the opportunity is now present for those who are able to go out and follow Smith's trail exactly. We look forward to their reports, and to an even greater understanding of what obstacles Jedediah had to surmount on his way to becoming one of the great men in the American West.

In addition to the Jennewein Collection and Todd Berens, I wish to thank the Missouri Historical Society, most particularly Mrs. Ernst A. Stadler, archivist, and Mrs. Fred C. Harrington, Jr., librarian. Mr. William G. Pettus, Jr., of St. Louis also deserves special mention. The Reverend Francis J. Weber of the Chancery Archives in Los Angeles, Dr. William A. Weber of the University of Colorado in Boulder, and Mr. Hermann R. Friis of the National Archives in Washington were most helpful with their assistance when it was requested. Mrs. James F. McGee of St. Louis assisted in making the first typescript of a difficult text, and Mrs. Ruth W. Fahey of Sturgeon Bay, Wisconsin, typed the final manuscript. There is, in addition, a host of long-suffering friends who tolerated their curiosity and my silence as I worked on a mysterious project.

"RAIBROOK"
Sturgeon Bay, Wisconsin
September 1976

The Journal of
Jedediah Strong Smith

The Journal

August 7th 1826 at our rendezvous at a place known as
the bend of Bear River.[1] My Partners Messrs Jackson
& Sublette and myself came to the conclusion that in
order to Prosecute our Business advantageously it was
necessary that our company Should be divided. We had

---

[1] A location between the present towns of Georgetown and Soda Springs,
Idaho. Morgan's *Ashley* suggests the probability that there had been two
points of rendezvous in 1826. The first can now be defined as being at the
"Cache" on Blacksmith Fork just east of present Hyrum, Utah, and the second
on the Bear River in the vicinity of Georgetown. Robert Campbell, who was
with Ashley, states that: "We remained in Cache Valley only a couple of
weeks, long enough to complete the traffic with the trappers. After we left
Cache Valley, Jackson and Sublette met us on Bear river. Ashley then sold
out his interest in the fur trade to Smith, his partner, and to Jackson and
Sublette, the new firm being known as Smith, Jackson & Sublette." ("A Narrative of Col. Robert Campbell's Experiences in the Rocky Mountains Fur Trade
from 1825 to 1835," a dictation taken by William Fayel in 1870, the Campbell
Papers, Missouri Historical Society. Missouri Historical Society will hereafter
be cited as MHS.) The point on the Bear River would have been convenient to
all parties, as Ashley left afterwards to return to St. Louis via South Pass,
and Jackson and Sublette could have used the Thomas Fork route to reach
their fall hunting grounds. The agreement between Ashley and Smith, Jackson
& Sublette is dated July 18, 1826, so Smith was at this point at least by then.

at that time in all   men.[2] It was decided that Messrs
Jackson & Sublette should go north on to the waters of
Lewises River[3] and the Missouri with   men[4] and
that I should take the remainder of the men and go to
the South. Of the Country to the S & S W we knew
comparatively little our travels having not extended
more than 100 miles to the S and about the same distance to the South west.[5] What that great and unexplored country might contain we knew not but hoped to
find parts of the country as well stocked with Beaver as
some the waters of the Missouri which was perhaps
as much as we could reasonably expect. In taking the
charge of our S western Expedition I followed the bent
of my strong inclination to visit this unexplored country and unfold those hidden resources of wealth and
bring to light those wonders which I readily imagined
a country so extensive might contain. I must confess
that I had at that time a full share of that ambition (and
perhaps foolish ambition) which is common in a greater

---

[2] The exact number is left blank in the manuscript. 42 men were transferred
from Ashley & Smith to Smith, Jackson & Sublette according to a document
dated Oct. 13, 1830, in the Sublette Papers, MHS.

[3] The Snake River, originally called the Lewis. The Campbell dictation, for
one source, states that: "When Smith left for [the] Colorado, Jackson and
Sublette with myself ascended the Snake river and tributaries near the Three
Tetons and hunted along to the forks of the Missouri, following the Gallatin,
and we trapped along across the head waters of the Columbia."

[4] The exact number is left blank in the text. Apparently, however, Jackson
and Sublette had the greater portion of the engaged men with them.

[5] For a discussion of the trappers' exploration around the Great Salt Lake
see Morgan, *Ashley,* 147-48. Ashley's travels in 1825, of course, had taken him
into the area to the south and southeast of Cache Valley.

or less degree to all the active world. I wa[nted] [6] to be the first to view a country on which the eyes of a white man had never gazed and to follow the course of rivers that run through a new land.

Our arrangements being completed Messrs J & S moved on to the north and I struck of passing the Soda Spring [7] and along the pummice stone valley to a small fork of the Port Neuff River [8] Here I encamped for the purpose of drying meat as the Buffalo were quite plenty and in fine order. I was well aware that to the south as far as my acquaintance extended there was but little game and experience had learned me in many a severe lesson the necessity of providing a supply of provision for traveling in a gameless country. My Party consisted of 18 persons besides myself. Their names are as follows [9]

---

[6] The missing letters are occasioned by a small hole in the manuscript.

[7] The exact date of the separation of the parties cannot be determined. Smith implies that he parted from the others at the rendezvous point (on Aug. 7?) in which case Jackson and Sublette could have headed east as far as Thomas Fork, and then used that avenue north to Snake waters. An alternative is that they all traveled together as far west as Soda Springs, and then Jackson and Sublette turned north toward the sources of the Blackfoot River. This is the earliest known document, incidentally, to use the name "Soda Springs."

[8] Smith traveled not to a "small fork" but to the main Portneuf River where it flows south before making its great bend to the west, and his "Pummice Stone valley" is the lava country in the Portneuf Valley. He must have passed Alexander Crater, for it appears as "Crater" in the Burr map of 1839 where the surrounding region is described as of "volcanic appearance." (*See* Morgan and Wheat, *Smith's Maps.*) In an attempt to establish a chronology for this portion of the trip, it is suggested that Smith went to the Portneuf on August 8, hunted there from the 9th to the 11th, and then turned south.

Robeseau	half breed U Canada
Nipisang	of Nipisang Ind & B America
Marion	Umpquah Ind a slave
John	a slave
Manuel	native Mexican
Harrison G. Rogers	a Virginian
Martin McCoy	Kentuckian
Peter Ranney	E Frenchman
Arthur Black	Scotchman
John Gaither	Kentucky
John Hanna	Missouri
Abraham Laplant	Indianna
Emmenuel Lazarus	German
Robert Evans	ould Ireland
Silas Goble	Ohio
John Wilson	Scotland
Daniel Ferguson	Unknown
James Reed	New York

[9] The list of names poses somewhat of a problem for the number here given, eighteen, does not agree with other estimates previously known. In his letter of Dec. 16, 1826, to the U.S. Plenipotentiary at Mexico, Smith says, "I with thirteen men;" in another letter of July 12, 1827, to William Clark it is a "party of fifteen men." Both Governor Echneandia and Capt. W. H. Cunningham speak of Smith's arrival in California with a party of fourteen (Morgan, *Smith,* 331, 334, 413 n.5). In all probability the discrepancies can never be resolved, however of this particular list we can make the following disposition. Two men, Gobel and Evans, made the complete trip back to the rendezvous of 1827 with Smith. Five men left the party along the way as we shall see: Robeseau (sometimes in print as Reubascans or Reubaseau) along with Nipisang and Manuel (Eustavan) deserted in southwestern Utah; Daniel Ferguson remained at San Gabriel; and the troublesome John Wilson went to

I had 28 horses exclusive of those belonging to the free men.[10] I remained on Portneuff three days during which time the Party had dried three horse loads of most excellent meat. I then started for cache or willow valley [11] to which place I was under the necessity of

San José. The eleven others – Rogers, McCoy, Ranney, Black, Gaither, Hanna, Laplant, Lazarus, Reed, and John (and Marion?) – remained in northern California in 1827, and ultimately perished in the Umpqua massacre on July 14, 1828. Of this group, it should be mentioned that Peter Ranney was not, as has been supposed, a Negro. This error was first made by Harrison Dale, who misread the Rogers daybook II (Ashley Papers, MHS. There "Ranne" appears well up in a list of men with Smith in 1828, but at the bottom is John Peter Rans(a), followed by the notation "a man of couler." It seems likely that the John who appears in this list as a slave (Indian or Negro?) and John Peter Ransa are one and the same. The Ranney-Ransa confusion is suggested by the fact that "Peter Raney" appears twice on a list of Umpqua victims submitted by Smith, Jackson Sublette to William Clark in 1829 (Morgan, *Smith,* 341), but John Ransa is missing. There is also the curious reference to "one other" in the roster of slain submitted by Smith, Jackson & Sublette to the Secretary of War in 1830 (*Ibid.,* 345), a list which contains "Rannee" but no John Ransa. Apparently the "one other" is this elusive "man of couler." Also of interest is the appearance of Marion, the Umpqua, as has been noted in the foreword. It had been thought previously that Marion was the lad caught by Toussaint Maréchal (Marishall) on July 3, 1828, as recorded in Rogers daybook II; but it is now possible, if somewhat improbable, that Marion made the original trip with Smith. Neither John nor Marion appears among those drawing supplies in Rogers daybook I, although all others in the present list are mentioned. Apparently the status of the two in the party was well defined.

[10] Capt. Cunningham in his account of the Smith party in California mentions that "Out of 50 horses which they started with, they brought only 18 in with them; the others having died on the road for want of food and water." (Dale, *Ashley-Smith,* 214 n.429.) Smith's remarks about the "free men" raises the question as to whether any free trappers accompanied Smith for a while, or at all.

[11] Smith probably followed the route taken by Peter Skene Ogden and William Kittson in the spring of 1825 as described in David E. Miller (ed.), "Peter Skene Ogden's Journal of his Expedition to Utah, 1825," 159-86. (For

going to procure some things from our cache [12] and to make some repairs on our Guns for at that place we had a sett of Black smith tools.[13] crossing Bear River and making several days at quick traveling I arrived at the Cache on the 15th of August.[14] found every thing safe at the Cache had some coal Burned a forge erected and my work underway as fast a possible. took such things as I wanted from the Cache [15] and on the 18th of August [16] I struck over west on to the Big Salt Lake

---

complete citations of books and articles listed in the footnotes, please refer to the Bibliography.) Today, State Highway 34 and then U.S. Highway 91 approximate the trip down from Soda Springs to Blacksmith Fork. Ogden took more time because he was trapping beaver as he went along, but there is a good description of the territory both in the journal itself and in Miller's notes.

[12] It could well be that it is simply this particular cache of Ashley's goods which gave its name to Cache (or Willow) Valley rather than the episode of the fatal accident set forth in Beckwourth and Ferris. T. D. Bonner, *The Life and Adventures of James P. Beckwourth*, 96; and J. Cecil Alter (ed.), *Life in the Rocky Mountains 1830-1835, by Warren Angus Ferris*, 42-43.

[13] Hence the name Blacksmith Fork for the branch of the Bear River at that point.

[14] This date seems to be confirmed by the notation in Rogers daybook 1. It is possible for Smith to have left the Portneuf on Aug. 12, assuming he hunted there from the 9th to the 11th, and reached Blacksmith Fork on the 15th.

[15] See the notations in Rogers daybook 1 for a memorandum of goods taken from the cache.

[16] There is some question as to the exact date of departure. Smith in his letter of Dec. 12, 1827, says that he left on the 22nd "from the Great Salt Lake" (Morgan, *Smith,* 334). This might, however, be taken to mean from the general area and perhaps more specifically, as we shall see, from Utah Lake. Morgan fixes departure from the cache on Aug. 16, basing his conclusion on the fact that Rogers daybook 1 lists distribution of rum on the 15th, or the day before leaving (*Ibid.,* 195). However, the daybook records that rum was also doled out on the 16th, and that "Reubaseau" (Robeseau) had a horse shod on

then south crossing webers fork to the outlet of the Uta Lake then up the outlet to the Lake.* [17] (* No buffalo ever visit the Uta Lake in the vicinity are some Elk and deer.) On a creek in the vicinity found some Beaver Sign and near by some Indians of the Uta nation.[18] Understanding by them that the principal Chief [19] with his band was not far off I sent an Indian for him. I was anxious to see him and if possible persuade him to make a treaty with the snake Indians for they had been constantly at war. I likewise wished to procure some information as to the Country to the South. In two days the

---

the 18th. The entry about the rum on the 16th certainly means that Smith would not have departed before the 17th, and the notation about the horse possibly suggests a last-minute repair at the forge before departure. On the basis of these suppositions, the 18th seems a perfectly acceptable date for departure although it means a rather forced trek to Utah Lake. The 17th, however, need not be ruled out; the horse may have required shoeing the first day out.

[17] This section of the trip takes Smith out of Cache Valley, probably by the old Sardine Canyon route rather than that slightly to the northwest used by the modern highway, U.S. 89-91. Smith then pursues a course down Box Elder Canyon, essentially that of the highway, to Brigham City where he turns south, crosses the Weber River, and moves up the "outlet" (named the Jordan River by the Mormons in 1847) to Utah Lake.

[18] The creek is most likely the Provo River, and the Ute Indian camp was somewhere in the vicinity of present Provo, Utah.

[19] The chief must have been Conmarrowap who figures in the Warren Ferris accounts of 1834-1835. For biographical notes on the chief *see* Dale L. Morgan and Eleanor Towles Harris (eds.), *The Rocky Mountain Journals of William Marshall Anderson – The West in 1834,* 290-91. This reference mentions a Mexican report which may allude to the treaty Smith concluded with him on this trip. A purported photograph of Conmarrowap which appears opposite page 96 in the Utah Hist. Qly., IX, 1-2 (Jan.-Apr. 1941) should be discounted.

Indian returned.[20] But the Chief could not be persuaded to come. He was afraid to leave his Band on account of the snakes who he was aprehensive might take the opportunity of his absence to make an attack. He sent word that if Beaver hunting was my object I had better pass his village as there were a good many beaver a short distance beyond where he then was. This I concluded to do and after three days travel from the Lake I arrived at his village on the 23d of August.[21] The country through which we travelled was quite rough and mountainous. I found at that place about 35 lodges some of Skins and some of Brush. Each family has 4 or 5 horses. These Indians are constantly moving about like the snakes and at this time live almost entirely on Service Berries which are now ripe. I remained at this place Two days and concluded a treaty with these Indians by which the americans are allowed to hunt & trap in and pass through their country unmolested and the chief after mature deliberation declared he would go thus far towards making peace with the snakes that hostilities on his part should cease.[22] I then told him

---

[20] Probably Aug. 21 and 22, 1826. Rogers daybook 1 records presents to the Utes made on Aug. 22, probably at some ceremony on the day prior to Smith's departure to visit Conmarrowap. Such a chronology would place Smith's arrival at the Ute camp on the Provo on Aug. 20.

[21] The date is more likely the 25th, assuming that Smith departed from the first Ute camp on the 23rd. He later says that he stayed with the chief for two days, presumably the 26th and 27th. Rogers daybook 1 records presents given the Indians on the 27th, the probable date of the treaty. The problem of where Smith met with Conmarrowap will be discussed shortly.

[22] The treaty is mentioned in the report sent to William Clark by Smith,

that the Snakes had consented to an armistice until a
meeting could be had between the two nations which on
my return from my fall hunt I engaged to forward by
every means in my power. I found these Indians more
honest than any I had ever been with in the country.[23]
They appear to have verry little disposition to steal and
ask for nothing unless it may be a little meat. As stealing and Begging are the most degrading features in the
Indian character and as their prevalence is almost uni-
versal so to be exempt from then is no ordinary merit.
The Uta's are cleanly quiet and active and make a
nearer approach to civilized life than any Indians I
have seen in the Interior. Their leggings and shirts
which are made of the skins of the Deer Mt Sheep or
Antelope are kept quite clean. As they sometimes visit
the Buffalo Country they have robes. Their arms are
like those of the Mountain Snakes Elk and Sheep horn
Bows. Having some communication with the Spanish
villages of Taos and Santa fee they have more guns than
the snakes. At this place I saw a display of that savage
disposition too prevalent among Indians. In camp were

Jackson & Sublette on [Dec.] 24, 1829, which in describing Smith's journey of
1827 says ". . . he passed the Utaw Indians with whom he had concluded
a treaty the year before. . ." (Morgan, *Smith*, 337).

[23] The Daniel Potts letter of July 8, 1827, describes his meeting with the
Utes in the spring of that year; Potts found them ". . . almost as numerous
as the Buffaloe on the prairis, and an exception to all human kind, for their
honesty." (*Ibid.*, 227). Potts, on his journey to the Sevier River, traveled
directly south from Utah Lake and did not go east into the mountains. Smith
was to follow Potts' footsteps when he again headed for California after the
1827 rendezvous.

two Snake women just taken. One of them was brought by a party which came in with me. She was not more than 13 or fourteen years of age. Light complexion and tolerable good features. She was obliged to sleep with her master every night and carry his pack by day and as there was no game in the country she had to dig roots for his food. This barbarous treatment would have passed perhaps unnoticed (for it is common to all Barbarians) had it not been for the result which had the effect to fix it on my mind. As soon as we arrived at the village she was delivered to the squaws in company with one brought in from another direction.[24] I made them a handsome present having been directed to do so by Genl. Ashley who acted in the capacity of a sub agent.[25] I purchased 3 horses for which I paid a high price. Of the country to the South no satisfactory information could be obtained But 20 or 30 miles to the East they told me there were some Beaver. I determined to move on E having been at this place 2 days.[26] The Indians

---

[24] These two Snake women were apparently purchased by Smith, or perhaps by Manuel Eustavan. The Rogers daybook 1 entry for Aug. 28 lists $27.00 in trade goods taken out by Manuel who could have then used the material to acquire the women. On Aug. 30, Manuel again goes into debt for a $3.00 black silk handkerchief, perhaps a present for one of his new-found friends. Later in the manuscript, in mentioning Manuel's desertion, Smith says that "The two snake women that I had purchased from the Utas to save them from the torture also ran off with him;" however, the Rogers entries imply that Manuel was, in fact, the purchaser.

[25] Rogers daybook 1 entry for Aug. 27 gives a list of the presents.

[26] As Smith prepares to leave the Utes, we must consider the first serious problem posed by this manuscript, that of where he actually found Conmarrowap, and the route of the expedition between Utah Lake and Castle Valley.

A village of 35 lodges represents a considerable encampment, but about all we can learn from Smith's text is that the Utes were somewhere in the mountains east of the lake havesting service berries. Smith's description of reaching them by traveling over a country "quite rough and mountainous" is certainly not specific enough to be of any help, but an examination of his journey after leaving the Indians suggests a possible route, even if it cannot locate the village site.

The course which agrees most nearly with Smith's description is one which would take him over a branch of the Spanish trail up Spanish Fork and along Soldier Creek, possibly as far as present Tucker, Utah, for his meeting with Conmarrowap. Allowing a starting point near Provo, this journey could take three days, for John C. Frémont used almost the same length of time to traverse the distance between Spanish Fork and Soldier Summit in 1844. The first day after leaving the chief's encampment, Smith and the Utes travel through a "country extremely rough until ascending a considerable Mt we kept on the top of a ridge running Eastwardly." This is here assumed to refer to the ascent of Soldier Creek to Soldier Summit, or perhaps along the ridge just north of this which is the watershed divide between the Great Basin and the Colorado River. Admittedly, the phrase "top of a ridge running Eastwardly" presents a problem, but such a formation does not really fit into any of the alternative routes either. Perhaps it is possible to reinforce Smith's account with the one given by Frémont in 1844: ". . . we reached the head of the stream [Soldier Creek]; and crossing, by an open and easy pass, the dividing ridge which separates the waters of the Great Basin from those of the Colorado, we reached the head branches of one of its larger tributaries, which, from the decided color of its water, has received the name of White river." (John Charles Frémont, *Report of the Exploring Expedition to the Rocky Mountains in the year 1842, and to Oregon and North California in the Years 1843-44*, 278). Beyond this point, after leaving the Indians, Smith finds a "valley and a creek about 20 yds wide running North East." Again we are faced with difficulties, for the White and Price rivers run *south* east; however, in view of the fact that the manuscript contains other directional errors, we might assume that this is one also, for the Price is the only stream in the area large enough to answer Smith's description.

Other alternatives may be considered, but they are less satisfactory. The Indians, for example, might have been near the headwaters of Diamond Fork, which could be reached either via Spanish Fork or Hobble Creek, but if Smith met them there, any projected course after he leaves them runs into serious trouble. He could have followed, more or less, the old Escalante route of 1776,

moved on in the same direction and encamped with me the first night. The country extremely rough until ascending a considerable Mt we kept on the top of a ridge running Eastwardly.[27] The next day I left the indians and proceeding onwards a few miles came to a valley and a Creek about 20 yds wide running North East.[28] At that place were some Beaver, so I remained there trapping 2 or 3 days. At this place I saw some verry old Buffalo sculls and from their appearance I

---

gone along the Strawberry River and then turned south up Avintaquin Canyon (the waters there run northeast, but they are small), but the "ridge running Eastwardly" does not materialize, and Smith's descriptions, scant as they are, do not match the region. Another possibility is that Smith went up Spanish Fork but turned south along Thistle Creek toward the Sanpete Valley, another favorite Indian haunt, and met the Utes someplace near present Indianola. He would then cross the Wasatch Plateau, a terrain fitting his "roughness" and "considerable Mt," and fall in with the Price where it does run northeast below present Scofield Reservoir, or perhaps keep going on over Ford Ridge west of Castle Gate to the river. This route is at best a tortuous and difficult one, ingenious but somewhat impractical.

No definite statement can be made about Smith's route on the basis of his account or because of our lack of knowledge of Conmarrowap's whereabouts. However, the Spanish Fork – Soldier Summit trail comes closest to what Smith suggests, and is a simple and basic route which follows the path of least resistance. It fits, that is, if one substitutes "southeast" for "northeast" as the direction of the river, and that substitution seems necessary.

As a final note, it might be mentioned that the pencil version of Smith's 1826 route on the Gibbs map (*see* Morgan and Wheat, *Smith's Maps*) suggests the great semicircular route swinging east through Castle Valley, and west to the Sevier. As overlaid on the printed map, however, it commences farther north, around Hobble Creek rather than Spanish Fork, but this could well be an error of transcription.

[27] The ridge is here proposed as that at Soldier Summit, Utah.

[28] Allowing for the presumed directional error in the text, this would be the White, and more importantly, the Price.

would suppose that it is many years since the Buffalo left this country. they are not found beyond this place.[29] I then moved on South having a high range of Mountains on the West and crossing a good many small streams running East into a large valley the valley of the Colorado.[30] But having learned that the valley was verry barren and Rocky I did not venture into it. The country is here extremely rough little appearance of Indians and game quite scarce a few Mt Sheep and Antelope. after traveling in this direction 2 days the country looked so unpromising that I determined to strike westward to a low place in the Mountain and cross over.[31] In crossing this mountain just as we were encamping I found an old squaw. (there had been several families at the place but they had run off at our approach). I prevailed on her to come to camp and one of the men gave her a Badger which I supposed she would take home to cook and eat. But the moment it was presented she caught it in her hands and exclaimed

---

[29] A pencil notation "Limit of Buffalo" appears on the Gibbs map at some distance northeast of Smith's 1826 route, in the Uinta Basin. Warren Ferris has some comments on the presence of buffalo in Utah in the mid-1820s (*see* J. Cecil Alter [ed.]; "W. A. Ferris in Utah 1830-1835," 81-108).

[30] Smith and his party turn away from the Price River and move southwest through Castle Valley, approximating the route of present Highway 10, keeping the Wasatch Plateau to the west. The exact chronology of the journey now becomes difficult to follow except for specific date entries in the Rogers daybook 1 that can be related to Smith's text.

[31] The route Smith takes through Castle Valley eventually falls in with the old Spanish Trail around Castle Dale, a route later to be followed in 1853 by the Beale, Gunnison, and Frémont expeditions. Smith turns west to cross the mountains at Ivie Creek, as does Highway 10 today.

we are all friends* (*These indians speak a language similar to the Uta's and as I had men in my party that spoke the Uta I was enabled to hold some conversation with them. They call themselves Sanpach.) and immediately tore it in pieces and laid it on the coals. When it was about half cooked she commenced eating making no nice distinction between hair pelts entrails and meet. When she had finished her meal I made her some trifling presents and told her to go and tell her people that we were all friends and that I should be glad to see some of them. She left us and in the evening some men came to the camp. I gave them some presents and by enquiry heard of a river to the west and engaged one of them as a guide.[32] After traveling three days from the place where I turned westward I came to the River of which the indian had spoken it was about 60 yds wide muddy water and runs N W.[33] This river I named Ashleys river in compliment to my friend the enter-

---

[32] There is no record in Rogers daybook I of these presents to the Sanpach (Sampatch) Indians.

[33] In traversing the mountains, Smith probably stayed to the south of the Salina Creek route now used by Highway 10, and chose, as did the branch of the Spanish Trail, and later Beale and Gunnison, to avoid the canyon. For descriptions of the terrain in 1853 *see* Gwinn Harris Heap, *Central Route to the Pacific, with related material on railroad explorations, etc. . . . 1853-1854* (edited by LeRoy R. and Ann W. Hafen), 215-18; and E. G. Beckwith, "Report of Exploration for a Route for the Pacific Railroad, by Capt. J. W. Gunnison, etc. . . ," in *Reports of Explorations and Surveys to Ascertain the most Practical and Economical Route for a Railroad from the Mississippi River to the Pacific Ocean,* II, 65-69. Hereafter the series will be cited as the *Pacific Railroad Surveys.*

prising Genl. W H Ashley.[34] Here I found some Beaver
sign. The Indians at this place are rather above the
midling size but in the mental scale lower than any
I have yet seen. Their dress of Leggings and shirts is
made of the skins of Deer Antelope and Mountain
Sheep. In appearance and action they are strongly contrasted with the cleanliness of the Uta's. The inhabitants of this river are the two tribes of Pa-utch and
Sam-pach. They appear to subsist entirely on Roots.
The principal one is about the size of a parsnip with
a leaf somewhat like the beat it grows on the richest
upland.[35] They prepare them by laying them on heated
Stones and covering them first with grass and then with
earth where they remain until they are sufficiently
steamed. They are then mashed fine and made into
small cakes. For their winter provision they are dried.
The language of the Uta's Sampach and Pa utch is
similar.

I had not as good Luck in taking beaver at this place
as I had expected from the sign. After remaining a day
or two I moved on two short days travel up the River
nearly N W [36] the valley being 6 or 8 miles wide and

[34] The Sevier River, which derives its present name from a corruption of
the Spanish "Rio Severo."

[35] It was the dependence of the Pa-utch (Pai-utes) on roots that led them to
be called "diggers," a term which was later used throughout much of the west
to describe root eaters.

[36] This is another example of a directional error in the text. Had Smith
traveled northwest he would have gone *down* the Sevier, not up, and would
have had to double back on his course.

covered with Sedge and But little grass except along the river. A few antelope but verry wild. Here I first saw the Black tailed hare.[37] Darker colored and not quite as large as the common hare. The Indians of this river are not numerous and may well be called wild for we seldom get sight of them.[38] They have a peculiar method of conveying intelligence of the approach of danger. Each family or set of families has a quantity of dry Sedge Bark and Brush piled up near the habitation and immediately on the approach of a Stranger they set fire to the pile and this being seen by their neighbor he does the same and the next the same so that the alarm flies

---

[37] In 1827 Daniel Potts tried to give the Sevier the name "Rabbit River," on account of the great number of large black tail rabbits or hares found in its vicinity." (Morgan, *Smith,* 226, in a quotation from Potts' letter of July 8, 1827).

[38] It might be well to mention at this point one of the problems in chronology encountered in the present text. Assuming that Smith made his treaty with Conmarrowap on Aug. 27, we can develop the following possible itinerary based on his account: Aug. 28, travels up Soldier Creek to Soldier Summit; Aug. 29, enters the White-Price Valley; Aug. 30-31, traps "2 or 3 days" on the Price; Sept. 1 and 2; goes through Castle Valley; Sept. 3, 4, and 5, crosses the Wasatch Mountains to the Sevier; Sept. 5 and 6, near present Salina, Utah; Sept. 7 and 8, moves up the Sevier. Even allowing for one or two days' leeway to accommodate such vague references as "2 or 3 days," it is probable that Smith was in the Sevier Valley or near it on Sept. 8, the date when Rogers daybook 1 lists "Indian present 1 Small Green handle knife." Because of the Rogers date, and the fact that Smith in describing his 1827 journey states: "At Lost River [Beaver River] the indians who were so wild when I passed the year before came to me by dozens. Every little party told me by Signs and words so that I could understand them, of the party of White Men that had passed the year before, having left a knife and other articles . . ." (Sullivan, *Travels,* 27) it has been assumed (Morgan, *Smith,* 196-97) that Smith had reached the Beaver by Sept. 8.

over the hills in every direction with the greatest rapidity. As soon as they have apprised their neighbor of the approaching danger they take every thing they possess (which by the by is not much their provision being secreted) and throw it into a large Basket shaped like a sugar Loaf with a strap attached to the top which comes across the forehead and with the Basket on their back away they run to the hills for security ——— As the Beaver were scarce and wild I determined to to move on south again. Just above where I left the river a range of high hills cross the valley.[39] I ascended a small creek coming in on the west side and at its head crossed a range of Mts and 3d short days travel Brought me into a low country on the west side of the Mt.[40] some small streams flowing from the Mt which I had crossed and running West I followed down and was not a little surprised to find that they all sunk in the sand.[41] As it

[39] Smith follows the Sevier up to the point where the mountains which form Marysvale Canyon close across the valley; he turns west here as he was to do again in 1827.

It was along the Sevier on his second trip that Smith found "tracks of horses and mules which appeared to have passed in the spring when the ground was soft," evidence which confirmed what the Utes had told him a few days previous of a band of starving trappers returning to Taos (Sullivan, *Travels*, 27). This group was a portion of the Ewing Young party which had reached the Colorado River by way of the Gila and was at the Mohave villages only shortly after Smith had departed for California (Morgan, *Smith*, 237-39).

[40] Proceeding up Clear Creek, Smith follows the route now taken by Highway 13, and after crossing the mountain range, emerges from it down Cove Creek near the present site of Cove Fort.

[41] This first abortive excursion probabliy takes Smith along the waters of Cove Creek for a short while until he discovered the futility of this course.

was useless for me to look for Beaver where there was no water I retraced my steps to where there was water and grass and encamped. On the following morning I started early and as the country look lowest to the S W we moved in that direction about 20 miles and to my great Surprise instead of a River an immense sand plain was before me where the utmost view with my Glass could not embrace any appearance of water. The only exception to this interminable waste of sand was a few detached rocky hills that rose from the surrounding plain and the stunted sedge that was thinly scattered over its surface. As it would not be advisable for me to push into a country of this description I retraced my steps and at a late hour at night found water near where I had encamped the night before.[42] Several of my horses gave out before encamping and were left. The next day I sent back for the horses that were left the party remaining in the same camp I started early on a good horse to take a view of the country travelling South. The range of mt which I had crossed in coming from Ashleys R extended South becoming in that direction somewhat higher. They may be considered the verge of the desert on the East other boundaries remaining as yet undefined. I went about 15 miles and from a high hill with my Glass could discover trees where I supposed

---

[42] On the second day in the vicinity of Cove Fort, Smith and his party venture farther afield and penetrate slightly into the Escalante Desert, and look out over the generally unpromising prospects of Beaver Bottoms and the basin of Sevier Lake before returning to his previous encampment.

there must be a stream running from the Mt W so I returned to camp.[43] The horses had been brought in in the course of the day and two or three Antelope had been killed. The next day made an early start and after a long days travel arrived at the place where I had seen the timber. Here I found a creek 20 yds wide running West with some little Beaver sign.[44] The smoke telegraph was seen on the hills during the day as usual. There had it appeared been a good many families in the vicinity but they had fled not desiring to become acquainted with us. Two Indians had remained behind to gratify their curiosity trusting to their speed perhaps for safety. But the poor fellows were quick undeceived when two men on swift horses pursued them. The probability is they had never seen or heard of horses before and of course were much frightened when they saw the men as it seemed to them sailing through the air. when overtaken nothing could be learned from them. They wanted no conversation with us personal safety was their only object. They feared they were about to pay for their curiosity with their lives but did not attempt to defend themselves and endeavored to express by a continued gabering and signs their desire that my men should go one way and they would go the other. finding

---

[43] On this particular day, Smith turns south on a course now used by Highway 91, and probably goes about as far as Gillies Hill before he catches sight of the trees ahead.

[44] This would be the Beaver River at the point where it issues from the mountains near Beaver, Utah.

it impossible to persuade them to come to camp I gave them some small presents and granted what appeared to be their greatest and only desire permission to leave us.[45] I trapped on this stream 2 or 3 days and moved down it some distance. But as there was no Beaver and the water began to fail and was apparently soon lost in the sand I ascended it again to the foot of the mountain and struck south again.[46] The stream I had left I called Lost Creek. Leaving lost Creek I traveled over some verry rocky hills for ten miles I then entered a valley which run a little west of south varying from 3 to 7 miles in width and followed down this about 20 miles before we found water.[47] It was late before the party all got up. Robeseau and Nipasang with their women and Boys left us today as they were anxious to go more East which I would not consent to do. At night Manuel one of my men ran off taking with him a horse Rifle

---

[45] Refer to note 38. These are the Indians to whom, it has been assumed, Smith gave the small green-handled knife mentioned in the Rogers daybook. Certainly the reference to presents here and in the 1827 account would tempt one to that conclusion, but the Rogers gift date of Sept. 8 does not fit. Picking up the chronology again, and based on statements made in this manuscript, it is possible the party spent Sept. 9, 10, and 11 following Clear Creek to Cove Fort, and on Sept. 12 they make their abortive push into the desert. Smith goes ahead to scout the trail to the south on Sept. 13, and the next day the entire party moves to the Beaver River.

[46] Like so many others after him, Smith is lured into following the Beaver (his Lost Creek) out into the Escalante Desert.

[47] Smith here enters the Parowan Valley, still following the route of modern Highway 91. He must have stayed close to the base of the Hurricane Cliffs on the east side of the valley because he does not mention Little Salt Lake. Apparently the camp that evening was in the vicinity of present Paragonah, Utah, or perhaps a little farther south near Parowan.

and ammunition belonging to the Comp.[48] The two
snake women that I had purchased from the Utas to
save them from the torture also ran off with him. This
was undoubtedly by his instigation as he could talk with
them which neither of my men could do he probably
told them he would take them to their own country.
A range of low mts still keeps on the E and on the W the
country has the same unwelcome appearance the detached hills are somewhat higher. In the plains are a

---

[48] It would be logical for the three men and their entourage to turn away
at this point and head back east toward the Sevier, for the main Spanish Trail
comes out of the mountains nearby. However, this reference to the desertion
needs further examination in view of the fact that both "Reubaseau" and
Neppasaing" appear in the Rogers daybook 1 entry for Sept. 22, and the
chronology as it is being developed from Smith's manuscript places the party
at this camp on or about Sept. 17 (allowing the 15th and 16th for trapping the
Beaver River, and the 17th for the trip to the Parowan Valley). Even if it is
assumed that the party was around Parowan on Sept. 22, the problem does not
resolve itself, for Smith in the present manuscript accounts for thirteen days
between his departure from this point and his arrival at Muddy River, and
the latter encampment is definitely pinned down by a Rogers entry: "Muddy
River Octr. 1st. 1826." Only eight days separate the 22nd from the 1st, so the
discrepancy of five days remains unsolved.

According to the schedule developed here, the Smith party would be on the
Virgin River at the Santa Clara (near modern St. George, Utah) on Sept. 22.
Sept. 18 and 19 are taken up by travel "south 2 days' 'through Parowan and
Cedar Valleys; Sept. 20 spent in going up Ash Creek and down to the Virgin;
and Sept. 21 and 22 passed on the Virgin going to the Santa Clara where the
group recruit for three days.

Two alternatives then present themselves: first, that the trio did desert in
the Parowan Valley and Smith is correct and Rogers wrong; or second, that
the men left on or about Sept. 22 from the Santa Clara camp, in which case
Rogers is correct and Smith in error.

Robeseau (Reubaseau), incidentally, went out again with Smith in the 1827
expedition; that time he made the entire journey, only to perish in the fight at
the Mohave villages. Perhaps his fears were justified.

few antelope and in the Mt some Ibex our dried meat
was now gone. In continuing South for 2 days a similar
country to the last described.[49] Small streams of water
coming out of the Mt on the E are soon lost in the Plain
on these creeks there is some grass and Brush. 2 or 3
antelopes killed. Came to a small Creek running S
followed it a part of a day but the country becoming
verry Rock and hilly I was obliged to turn off to the
right where after traveling 8 or 10 miles through a
rough country I came to a stream about 60 yds wide
running S W and coming from the N E: consequently
it must head with Ashleys River.[50] This river I call
Adam's River in honor of the present President.[51] I pro-
ceded on down this river and as we found no game or
Beaver we had nothing to eat. The grass of the river at
this place was of those coarse tough kinds which we call
Salt and Cane grass. On the day after I struck the river

---

[49] During these two days, the party is going south through the Parowan and
Cedar Valleys, probably staying close to the base of the Hurricane Cliffs on
the east, as does present Highway 91.

[50] Finding the route of his small creek (Ash Creek) troublesome, Smith
turns to the southwest in the vicinity of present Anderson Ranch. From this
point there are two possible approaches to the Virgin: the first would take the
party briefly southwest and then due south along Dipping Pen Wash, east of
which today there is a jeep trail; the second would have the party continue
farther along to the southwest to present Harrisburg where it would then turn
left and follow Quail Creek to the river. The description of rough country
would satisfy either alternative. Smith is correct here in assuming that the
Virgin heads with the Sevier.

[51] Although Smith's tribute to John Quincy Adams is identified with the
river in some early maps, the name Virgin (Rio Virgen) was commonly
accepted after it was popularized by Frémont.

I passed a small spot of ground where corn had been raised 3 or 4 years since. Some of my men could hardly believe it possible that corn had ever been planted in this lonely country although the remains of the stalks were found. The hills being irregular convinced me that it was the work of Indians. The course of the River which is wide sandy and shallow continues S W and the country off from the River Rough Rocky & Red hills no timber or game.[52] On the evening of the second day I had advanced a little ahead of the company to look for a place to encamp. near a small Creek[53] coming in from the west and at the distance of 200 yeards I observed an Indian on a hill and made signs for him to come to me but he presented his bow and arrows and in a moment I saw 15 or 20 appear. not considering it safe to remain here I hastened back to the party and then proceeded on to the selected encampment. By this time 20 or 30 were seen skulking around among the Rocks.[54] I therefore had every thing prepared for the worst and advancing alone before the camp by making signs and speaking in a friendly tone of voice I finally succeeded in persuading one of them to come to me.

---

[52] Smith is now in red earth country; the Vermillion Cliffs, for example, lie some twenty miles to the east.

[53] This creek is the Santa Clara River, often called by Smith, "Corn Creek." Based on the chronology which is herein attempted, the date of arrival would have been about Sept. 22, 1826.

[54] The Indians encountered were some of the southern Paiutes, soon to be known also as "Diggers." They were later to harass passing travelers, and Frémont looked upon them as the "Arabs of the New World." (Frémont, 269).

The poor fellow the bravest in the band advanced with evident signs of fear his limbs trembling and his voice faltering. holding out in his hand a hare or rabbit to offer as a token of friendship. I took it and carrassed him and he immediately set down. When the others saw that he was not hurt 10 or 12 of them came bringing in their hands an ear of corn as an emblem of peace – (a pleasing sight to starving men) they set down Began to talk and make signs. As provisions was our greatest present desire we were much pleased to hear that they had corn and pumpkins close at hand.[55] I gave them some small presents among which I found that pieces of Iron were verry acceptable and started some of them off for corn & pumpkins. they soon returned well loaded and indiferent as this may seem to him who never made his pillow of the sand of the plain or him who would consider it a hardship to go without his dinner yet to us weary and hungry in the solitary desert it was a feast a treat that made my party in their sudden hilarity and Glee present a lively contrast to the moody desponding silence of the night before. As both men and horses required rest I thought it advisable to remain here 2 or three days[56] during which time I sent some men down

---

[55] Smith mentions in his letter to the Minister Plenipotentiary at Mexico that by this time the supply of dried buffalo meat which he had brought with him from the Portneuf was exhausted (Morgan, *Smith,* 331). In 1827, the site was deserted, for Smith relates "Not an indian was to be seen, neither was there any appearance of their having been there in the course of the summer their little Lodges were burned down." (Sullivan, *Travels,* 28).

[56] Although the itinerary as being developed suggests that Smith and his party reach the Santa Clara on Sept. 22, the flurry of activity recorded in

to the river to see what the prospect was ahead and 2 men back on the trail for 2 horses that had been left behind. In the mean time I was trading for Corn in order to have a small stock of provision when I started again. My men from below returned and told me that the river about 10 m below entered the mountain which we could see from camp and that we could not follow the River through the Mt unless we traveled in the water as the Rocks rise from the water perpendicularly on both sides.[57] The river being wide and shallow there is no chance for Beaver but there being a great many willows cut on the banks it appeared that they came here in high water and the Indians by signals told me that there were plenty below.[58] The two men returned on the third day with the tired horses. The weather while here was verry warm the Mercury rising above blood heat. I visited some indian lodges a mile above our camp on the creek for the purpose of seeing how they farm. Their little corn patch is close on the bank of the creek for the convenience of water. The Creek

Rogers daybook 1 on Sept. 21, 22, 23, and 24 may indicate a slightly earlier arrival. Most likely the Rogers dates refer to the period when the party remained at this camp.

[57] Smith's scouts advance as far south as the narrows which mark the beginning of the canyon of the Virgin River; the stream at that time of year would contain some water, although portions of the bed through the canyon were usually dry in summer.

[58] Smith later remarks that "it is a general characteristic of indians to answer your questions in the manner that they think will please you but without any regard to the truth." There were some beaver below the canyon around Beaver Dam Wash, but probably not in such numbers as to excite a person in the fur trade.

is damed about and the water is conducted in a trunk to a place where it can be spread over the surface. For a hoe they use a piece of wood 3 in Broad and 4 feet Long. The pumpkins and Corn were not quite ripe. Their small Lodges are covered with weeds and cane grass the fires being on the out side. They kept their women and children secreted so that I did not see one while with them. They have some Crockery which is thiner than common Brown earthen colored yellow lead Color and like stone ware. I saw no Iron among them so that any piece that could be converted into a knife or an arrow point was a great acquisition. They have pipes made of fine clouded marble[59] and a kind of Tobacco of their own like that which we in the Mountains call snake Tobacco. Each man smokes for himself not passing the pipe around the circle as is the custom among the Mt Indians. They care verry little about our Tobacco. A good many of these Indians were the scalp of an antelope or Mt sheep with the ears on for a hat. In actions and language these indians are like the Pa utch.* (* From the place where I struck Adams River to Corn Creek[60] there was but a few places where there was any timber. What I saw was cotton wood and in places willows The grasses were Cane salt and wire grass. On Corn Creek was a considerable Cotton wood

---

[59] One of the pipes was obtained by Smith as a present for General William Clark: "The *Pa Ulches* have a number of marble pipes, one of which I obtained and send you, altho' it has been broken since I have had it in my possession. . ." Smith to Clark, July 12, 1827, quoted in Morgan, *Smith,* 335.

[60] *i.e.* the Santa Clara.

& willows. The country on the Adams River above where I struck it had a peculiarly wild and rugged appearance. I found two or three shrubs that were new to me. On growing in bundles like a currant bush with a bright red and polished bark. Another about three feet high green bark prickly surface and when striped of the bark is perforated it is hollow like a reed.[61]) Having somewhat recruited both men and horses I moved on down the River to the foot of the Mt and then turned off to the right[62] the course of the river still S W winding about among the rocks and ravines. I succeeded in gaining the Summit of the Mt composed of Ridges of Rock and gravel. But although I was so high that I could see the low ground beyond the mountain yet there was a deep ravine before me which I was

[61] William A. Weber, Professor of Botany and Curator of the Univ. of Colo. Museum, has been kind enough to furnish identification of the plants. According to him, the one which Smith described as resembling a currant and having red bark "would be the *Arctostaphylos pringlei* Parry, commonly called 'Manzanita,'" and the other with the green bark "has to be a species of *Opuntia* in the Cylindropuntia group, most likely *Opuntia acanthocarpa* Engelm. & Bigelow."

[62] It would appear that the party continues down the Virgin at least as far as the Bloomington-Atkinville area before turning west up into the hills, possibly around Curly Hollow Wash, and then abandons this route to return to the river along West Mountain Valley Wash which would bring them into the Big Round Valley just above the First Narrows. In 1827, Smith avoided the difficulties of a transit of the canyon by continuing on up the Santa Clara, crossing the mountains at Castle Cliff Wash, and returning to the Virgin along Beaver Dam Wash, following the approximate route of present Highway 91. Once and for all, if it is still necessary, the present account puts to rest the Meadow Valley Wash – Muddy River route theorized by C. Hart Merriam in "Earliest Crossing of the Deserts of Utah and Nevada to Southern California: Route of Jedediah S. Smith in 1826," 228-36.

obliged to cross the descent was extremely steep and as we had had no water since morning I was obliged to follow down the Ravine to the River & as it was then nearly night encamped without any grass for my horses. I killed an Ibex in good order and one of the men killed another. These relished verry well with men who had been for several days deprived of their accustomed rations of meat. Early the next morning we started down in the bed of the general shallowness of the water. By the meanderings of the stream it was about 12 m through the rocks rising perpendicularly from the waters edge in most places to the heighth of 3 or 400 feet. A good many hot springs but not as hot as some I have seen at the Salt Lake and on the Big horn.[63] Some appearance of Iron ore. At one place I was obliged to unload and swim the horses.[64] Moved about 3 miles after getting through the mountain to the bed of a stream coming in from the west on which there was some good sized cotton wood trees.[65] There is verry little appearance of Indians in this vicinity. The country is not so rough as on the other side of the mountain but extremely barren and the river continues wide and

---

[63] These hot springs seem to have escaped the attention of others who have described the canyon of the Virgin.

[64] This confirms the indication of a crossing of the Virgin which was earlier deduced from the Burr Map of 1839 (Morgan and Wheat, *Smith's Maps*, 62). The party follows the north bank of the stream up to this point, and crosses back over near Muddy River.

[65] The stream is Beaver Dam Wash, which Smith used in 1827 to avoid the Virgin Canyon and which he then called Pautch Creek (Sullivan, *Travels*, 28).

shoal. At this place I saw a new kind of quail some smaller than the atlantic quail.[66] The male has three or four feathers an inch long rising from the top of the head. For four days traveling down the River nothing new or material occured. After passing the Mt the River turns more south keeping nearly parallel with the mountain and at the distance of 5 miles. The grass has been somewhat plentier along the river, and in two or three places a few small cotton wood trees. No game since we left the Mt. On the evening of the fourth day from the Mt I saw an Indian at a distance called to him and after a little hesitation he came to me and understanding by his signals that there was some lodges near by we went on to the mouth of a creek from the SW small but apparently unfailing on the bank of which was several Lodges of Indians like those on corn Creek.[67] They had corn (which was gathered) Pumpkins squashes and some small green Water Melons. I soon purchased some pumpkins and squashes and encamped. As I was weary of traveling in this barren

[66] The bird is Gambel's Quail (*Lophortyx gambeli*) which closely resembles the California quail, but replaces it in desert areas. *See* Roger Tory Peterson, *A Field Guide to Western Birds*, 67.

[67] Smith has now reached the Muddy River, by which name the stream appears in the Rogers daybook I entries for Oct. 1 and 2, 1826. Those dates conform with the chronology as it is unfolding. The party leaves the Santa Clara on Sept. 25 for their detour into the mountains; the next day is spent on going through the canyon to Beaver Dam Wash. Sept. 27-30 represent the four days "from the Mt" which brings the group to the Muddy. There is an error, again, in the text about direction, the Muddy comes into the Virgin from the northwest. The whole area today is inundated by Lake Mead.

country I of course made many enquiries of the Indians as to the country ahead. They told me there was a large river not far off and of course plenty of Beaver for it is a general characteristic of indians to answer your questions in the manner that they think will please you but without any regard to the truth. There are however some individuals of different tribes in the Mts on whose word you may depend. These Indians are Pa utch but not as wild as those above the Mt. their women and children did not run off. I saw at their Lodges a large cake of rock salt weighting 12 or 15 lbs and on enquiry found that they procured it a cave not far distant. I engaged an indian and sent one of my men to ascertain the truth. The men reported it as true. I saw Ochre among these Indians which was procured from the N E about 30 m. I thought I had some reason to believe these indians in relation to the beaver as they had mocasins made of the skins. It happened that there there were two indians here from another tribe apparently for the purpose of trading for salt and ochre.[68] They told me that a days travel below here this river entered another large River coming from the North East and several days journey Below the mouth of this river they resided where there is plenty of beaver and the indians have horses. I saw on these indians some blue yarn and

---

[68] From what few clues are given about these two Indians, it appears that they were Mohaves from the Cottonwood Valley area of the Colorado. They later desert Smith in some particularly rugged terrain just before reaching the valley.

a small piece or two of Iron from which I judged they had some intercourse with the Spanish provinces. I engaged these indians as guides for I might as well go on as undertake to return. Some of my horses had given out and were left and others were so poor as not to be able to carry a load. The prospect ahead was if the indians told me the truth that I might in this moderate Climate trap all winter and also purchase some horses. these considerations induced me to abandon the idea of returning to the mountains until I should have gone somewhat further in exploring the secrets of this thus far unpromising country.

Having stayed at the mouth of   [69] creek 2 days I started on down the river accompanied by my two guides when I was opposite the cave I turned off to the right across a level piece of ground about ½ mile to the foot of a hill which appears to be two or three mile long and 100 or 150 feet high its course being about parallel with the River which is here running S E or E S E.[70] Ascending from the foot of the hill 80 or 90 feet I arrived at the entranc of the cave which is about 15 feet high and the same width gradually close as I advanced

---

[69] The name of the creek is left blank in the text. Sullivan chose to insert "bitter" when he encountered similar gaps in the 1827 journal (Sullivan, *Travels,* 28).

[70] Before the creation of Lake Mead, the Virgin at this point flowed almost due south, or perhaps a little to the southwest. The error in direction as given by Smith may well be due to his ignoring a marked compass deviation (*Ibid.,* 166 n.52).

to 4 feet in width and 10 feet in heighth where it was quite difficult of descent for a short distance perhaps ten feet where you arrive on a floor the room then opens to about 15 or 18 feet in width 25 or 30 feet in length and 20 feet in heighth. The Roof sides and floor of solid rock salt. I had brought an axe for the purpose of examining it and on breaking it found it generally pure But in places a few dark veins.[71] after satisfying my curiosity I proceeded onwards a few miles and encamped.

The next day S E 15 m [72] to the large river of which my guides had spoken. It was about 200 yards wide [73] deep and a strong current. Coming from the N N E and from this place running south it could be no other but the Colorado of the west which in the Mountains we call seetes-kee-der. Up the River the country presents a hilly Barren appearance and below and all around Barren Stony hills. In some places are a few small trees

---

[71] This remarkable topographical landmark which Smith called "Adams cave" in his letter to the Minister Plenipotentiary at Mexico (Morgan, *Smith*, 332), was about three miles below the former town of St. Thomas, Utah, on the west bank of the Virgin. The cave now lies dissolved beneath the waters of Lake Mead, but such present shoreside names as Salt Point and Salt Bay refer to the general area of the site. Smith gathered a sample of the salt and later sent it on to William Clark (*Ibid.*, 335).

[72] Here again Smith's direction is wrong, for the river flowed nearly south. Assuming that the party leaves the Muddy on Oct. 3 and visits the salt cave that day, they arrive at and cross the Colorado on the 4th. The next day, as Smith mentions, the group remains in camp to avoid travel in the heat of the day; this would be the "Siskadee" camp listed on Oct. 5 in Rogers daybook I.

[73] There is a blank space in the text at this point.

along the bank of the Colorado. The guides said it would be necessary to cross the river at this place. I there formed a raft of drift wood on which to carry over my goods. The horses were driven in and crossed over after crossing all over moved down the River a mile and enc.[74] Where we crossed the river an Indian and his family were living.[75] They had pumpkins squashes and Beans growing on a small spot of alluvial soil on the River bank. I purchased of the different kinds and he showed me where he had wheat sown or rather planted in the hills 20 or 30 grains in the hill. The River entering a low but rugged mountain below [76] I found it would be necessary to turn off from it to the left and as my guides informed me that it was more than a days travel to the next accessible point on the river between which place and this no water could be found I determined to wait until the heat of the day was over and travel as much as possible in the night. At the proper time we moved on keeping a south East course up a wide gravelly ravine the course of which

---

74 In modern times, until the creation of Lake Mead, there was a ferry at the point used by Smith for the crossing. The party probably then proceeded to the base of Detrital Wash for their camp.

75 Smith was to meet this same "old Pautch farmer still on the east side of the Colorado" when he passed the spot on his next trip. (Sullivan, *Travels*, 28.)

76 Smith here refers to the Black Mountains, through which the Colorado runs west before making its great bend to the south around Fortification Hill. Joseph C. Ives, *Report upon the Colorado River of the West, Explored in 1857 and 1858* (Washington, 1861), offers perhaps the best description of the river in the condition in which it must have been in Smith's day.

was nearly parallel with the obstructing range of Mt.[77] At 11 or 12 o clock at night we unpacked and hobled our horses and slept untill the first appearance of light when we prepared and moved on for three hours in the direction of yesterday the Mt. then becoming lower we turned through a low place S S W and after traveling 2 hours more over terrible rocks we arrived at the river where although we found water which we verry much needed yet there was nothing for the hungry and weary horses to eat.[78] The indians had carried water in the bladder of an antelope which they divided with us yet it was nothing among so many. Just below camp the river again enters the rocks.

The next morning we started early leaving the river and traveling S E 4 or 5 miles up a ravine we got where the hills are fewer and more detached. The country of that same Barren and rough kind I have so often described. My guides had left me in the morning but I had been able to follow their tracks in the sand. The trail turning in toward the river through a range of rough hills by a narrow and deep ravin frequently obstructed by rocks I was apprehensive I would not be able to pass with my horses. As I was some distance ahead of the party and on foot I pushed on briskly

[77] Smith proceeds up Detrital Valley, along the wash, keeping Wilson Ridge of the Black Mountains on his right (west).

[78] Continuing on up Detrital Valley, the party probably turns west around the southern edge of Wilson Ridge at Householder Pass, and then follows a small wash down to the vicinity of present Willow Beach and the Colorado. The spot is approximately opposite Ives camp 58.

to see the worst. I found some verry difficulty places but seeing no other chance for proceeding after taking a drink from the River I returned to meet the company. They had been clamberring and winding among the rocks and were now about three miles from the river. Being now night and a place before us that would require some hours to pass I had the horses unpacked and left them as they could not go back on account of the steep places we had come down.[79]

One of the men who was so lame that he could not walk was obliged to remain while the party moved on to the river on foot. As soon as light the next day we returned and with cords lowered our goods down the precipice. where a mistep would have been in its consequences inevitable destruction.* (* It was at this place a party from Taos saw my trail.)[80] But fortunately we passed in

---

[79] Realizing that the Colorado was about to enter Black Canyon, Smith turns southeast up Jumbo Wash to the present site of Pope Mine. From there, as is suggested in Morgan and Wheat, *Smith's Maps*, 63, it is now apparent that the party follows a narrow canyon that runs almost due west to the river. In his journal of 1827, Smith says that "instead of taking the ravine in which I had so much difficulty, I took another further south and passed in to the river without difficulty." (Sullivan, *Travels*, 28.) The preferable route cannot be determined with any certainty, but it could be that in 1827 Smith went on a little south from the Pope Mine area and followed the trail taken by a modern jeep road past Van Deemen Mine down to the river. Or he could have made a grand sweep of the whole area and returned to the Detrital Valley and then swung south of Mount Perkins to rejoin the Colorado in Cottonwood Valley.

[80] This could be a reference to the Ewing Young party (*see* note 39) which passed north along the Colorado after leaving the Mohave villages in the late winter of 1827.

Or, and this has greater significance, it might be an indication that Smith

safety and packing up pushed on to the river where there was a little grass for our horses. The next day I moved 10 miles down the river the hills not so bad as they had been heretofor. In the course of the day some indians met us having some dried pumpkins. finding tolerable grass I remained two days.[81] I killed a Mt sheep and we caught some pretty good fish with the

did indeed have an awareness of the band under Richard Campbell (who is usually accepted as having been with Young) which traveled from Taos to San Diego on a second trip later in 1827. *See* Alice B. Maloney, "The Richard Campbell Party of 1827," 347-54.

When Smith was in Monterey in the fall of 1827 on his second trip, he mentions that "news came in from the South that another party of Americans were near Too Larre Lake. I told [Governor Echeandia] I was well convin[c]ed there were no Americans there, but as it was his request, I would write to them." (Sullivan, *Travels,* 42.) This other party has since been identified as Campbell's; perhaps Smith did receive an answer to the letter, or he learned the identity of the men through a later meeting with a member of the expedition.

If this is a reference to Campbell, Smith's comments would be important in establishing Campbell in this area, for his route to California has never been definitely determined. Many have thought that he arrived at the Colorado River via the Gila, although Campbell himself later remembered the route as being more northern. One such alternative is presented by David J. Weber in *The Taos Trappers,* 134-6, and takes Campbell north of the Grand Canyon. Weber's book also contains much information on Ewing Young.

[81] Smith and his party arrive in Cottonwood Valley, an area now inundated by the waters of Lake Mohave since the construction of Davis Dam farther south. The travel from the mouth of the Virgin has taken five days (Oct. 5, up Detrital Wash; Oct. 6 at Willow Beach; Oct. 7 and 8, near the treacherous canyon; and Oct. 9, into Cottonwood Valley). This more or less confirms Smith's statement in this July 12, 1827, letter to William Clark that he "crossed the Seedskeeder, and went down it four days" to the Mohave villages. Smith probably meant the general area of the Indians, *i.e.* Cottonwood Valley where he first met them, rather than the Mohave Valley in particular. This travel time has been debated as being much too short (Morgan, *Smith,* 335).

hook and line. One of my men found a singular substance Some hard and transparent pieces of stone about twice as large as a large pea were firmly fixed in the side of a flat stone.[82] Appearance of an abundance of Iron ore are seen here. and most certainly if a country produces minerals in proportion to its barrenness this must be rich in mineral productions.

I had lost a good many horses and some of those remaining were not able to carry any thing. I got the Indians to assist me in moving down to where there was several lodges.[83] These Indians are quite a different nation from the Pa utch. They call themselves A-muc-ha-ba's [84] and appeared quite friendly bringing me corn beans dried pumpkins &c which I paid them for in Beeds Rings vermillion &c. At this place there is considerable timber on the river and the soil might admit of making small farms. There was but 3 or 4 horses among them but I did not succeed in purchasing them. verry little beaver

82 Lieutenant Joseph C. Ives of the Topographical Engineers explored the Colorado River in 1857 and 1858, and his report includes a rather detailed geological section which discusses the rocks in Cottonwood Valley more scientifically.

83 Smith at this point has moved farther down Cottonwood Valley.

84 The Mohave Indians. The ensuing account and description of the tribe is the first by an American. As Morgan has pointed out, other descriptions of the Indians approximately as Smith found them are in Elliott Coues (ed.), *On the Trail of a Spanish Pioneer*, I, 226-33, 308-12; L. Sitgreaves, *Report of an Expedition down the Zuni and Colorado Rivers*, 16-20; Lieutenant A. M. Whipple, "Report Upon a Route near the Thirty-Fifth Parallel," *Pacific Railroad Surveys*, III, 112-19; E. W. Beale, *Wagon Road from Fort Defiance to the Colorado River*, 74-6; and Ives, *Report Upon the Colorado*, 65-91. (*See* Morgan, *Smith*, 415 n.13.)

sign on the river. By enquiry I found that the principal part of this tribe were 30 or 40 miles down the river. I remained at this place 2 days during which time a number of Indians came up from the village below. Among these were one or two that could talk spanish and as I had a man that was able to speak the spanish I could hold some conversation with them.[85] I then moved on down the River accompanied by the Indians who had come up from the settlements below. The distance was upwards of thirty miles and the country barren. On my arrival at the settlement I was treated with great kindness.[86] Melons and roasted pumpkins were presented in great abundance – At this time it was low water yet the Colorado was 200 yards and in the shoalest place I could find 10 feet deep with a smooth current. The timber in this vicinity consisting of the Cottonwood and a small species of Honey Locust[87] with some willow extends entirely along the river varying in width from ½ to 2½ miles in width the river winding through woodland from one side to the other

---

[85] Probably Smith refers to Abraham Laplant. Later in this text Smith mentions a visit to Los Angeles and notes that "I went taking with me my interpreter." Rogers in his daybook 1 entry December, records in connection with the same excursion that "Mr. S. and Laplant returned."

[86] Smith now enters the Mohave Valley and encounters the main Mohave settlement. Oct. 15 is suggested as the date of arrival in our proposed itinerary. He remained two days, Oct. 10 and 11, in the northern portion of Cottonwood Valley; moved through it on the 12th; and stayed two days, Oct. 13 and 14, in the southern end of the valley "where there was several lodges." On the 15th he proceeded farther south on the Colorado to the Mohave Valley.

[87] The screw mesquite *(Prosopis pubescens)*, of which more later.

alternately. Leaving the woodland which has a tolerable soil the sandy region commences producing nothing but sedge and prickly pear. On the East and West at the distance of ten miles a chain of Rocky hills run parallel with the river and about thirty miles south the Rocky hills close in to the River.[88] This settlement of the Amuchaba's extending about 30 miles along the River appeared quite numerous and paying some considerable attention to agriculture they do not live in villages but are rather scattered over the country generaly whereever they find the most favorable situations.[89] In person these Indians are tall and well formed complexion not dark.[90] In abilities perhaps second to

---

[88] These would be the Black Mountains on the east; the Dead and Sacramento Mountains on the west; and the Chemehuevi to the South, through which the Colorado runs in the Mohave Canyon.

[89] Smith gives a remarkably incisive view of the life and customs of the Mohaves. Such is not surprising, of course, in view of his past experiences which alerted him to probing observations of Indians, but it does stand in contrast to other portions of this text in which he glosses over situations (his stay in San Diego, for example). In its own way this text offers as good a view of the Mohaves as that made by Lieutenant Amiel W. Whipple when he visited the valley in Feb., 1854. Certainly it is ethnologically superior to that of Lieutenant Joseph C. Ives (a member of the Whipple party) who spent two weeks among the Mohaves in Feb. 1858, while exploring the Colorado by steamboat with his own group. Smith's comments also compare favorably with those presented nearly a century later, in 1925, by Alfred Louis Kroeber in *Handbook of the Indians of California*. Kroeber, for instance, writes of the Mohaves' community life: "They do not think of its settlements . . . the village does not enter into the scheme . . . Their settlements were small, scattering, and perhaps only occupied for short times; the people all mixed freely with one another." (Kroeber, 727.)

[90] "The color of both sexes is distinctly yellowish – as often appears in the women when they wash –." (*Ibid.*, 728.)

the Utas. They do not appear much inclined to steal but are quite fond of gambling. Their principal Game is conducted as follows. A piece of ground 30 or 40 feet long and 8 feet wide is made level and smooth. Each man has a pole ten feet long and one of them a hoop 4 inches in diameter. The hoop is set rolling from one end of the floor and at the instant both start and sliding their poles endeavor to intersect the hoop. The one that pierces the hoop or when hoop and poles stop is the nearest to the spot is the winner.[91] The women also gamble by tossing small colored sticks in a dish somewhat like throwing dice. The women are generally very fleshy with tolerable features. The man when dressed at all have a Spanish Blanket thrown over the left shoulder and passing under the right arm it is pined on the breast with a wooden pin. They wear no head dress mocasins or leggings. The dress of the women is a peticoat made of a material like flax just Broken which is Banded with a plat on the upper edge like corn husks. It is fastened around the waist extending down to the knee and constitutes with whole of their clothing. They are in general much more cleanly than the Pautch.

---

[91] Kroeber gives a brief play-by-play of this game: "The favored game of the Mohaves was between two players, each of whom cast a long pole at a rolling hoop. The ring was thrown by the winner of the last point, and either runner was at liberty to dart his pole when he pleased. If the hoop was pierced, nothing was counted. If the ring rested on the pole with sufficient overlap that a space was visible, one point was made. Should the ring lie on the end of the pole, the score was double. If both players cast successfully, both scored. Four points won the stakes. A favorite device was to hurl one's pole between the opponent's and the hoop." (*Ibid.,* 748.)

They make a kind of earthen ware and in large crocks of this they boil their beans corn pumpkins &c. The men appear to work as much in the field as the women which is quite an unusual sight among Indians. But few of them have bows and arrows. The bows are 5 feet long and the arrows verry long and made of cane grass with a wooden splice 6 inches long for a head. It is fashion with these indians to fill the hair full of mud and wind it around the head until the top resembles in shap a tin pan. Their summer Lodges about 3 feet high are made of forks and poles covered with grass weeds [92] and dirt flat on the top. The winter Lodges generally small are made in the woods but fronting to the south and where the trees are not sufficiently high to keep out the sun.[93] As the rainy season approaches they throw dirt on the roof to give it a slope to carry off the water and also secure the sides with dirt leaving only a small aperture for a door. As they have not much clothing when the weather requires it they build a great many small fires sleeping in the intervals between them. When they become cold they draw the sand out from under fires and spread it where they sleep. In their Lodges I observed an abundance of Crocks and demijohns. Goards and small bins made of willow in which they put their corn, beans, wheat, garden seeds, and melons. The

---

[92] The arrow weed *(Pluchea sericea)* was the most common thatching medium *(Ibid., 731)*.

[93] For a description of Mohave housing, *see* Kroeber, 731-5. The doors apparently faced south because of the coldness of the north winds.

Honey Locust of this country bears a pod somewhat longer than a bean.[94] The Indians gather these and pound both the pod and the bean it contains until it forms a coarse flour. they work it into loaves and Let it dry it is then fit for use. When they use it they rinse it with water to which it imparts a sweet and yet tartish taste by no means unpleasant. I frequently observed at a distance from their houses willow bins that would hold 20 to 100 Bushels filled with the Locust pods from which circumstances I judged them not much inclined to steal from each other. Their method of grinding their wheat is somewhat tedious. On a large flat stone a little concave it is pounded or rather rolled with another stone in the shape of a bakers rolling pin until it is sufficiently fine.[95] The stone on which the grinding is done being placed in a sloping possition gradually as the meal becomes fine it is permitted to slide off into a dish at the lower end. The bread which they form of this meal is baked in the sand or ashes under the fire without the covering of Bark or grass used by the Pawnees. When they would roast their Pumpkins or

---

[94] Kroeber, 736-7, describes the process: "Mesquite beans are crushed with a stone pestle in a wooden mortar, the hard seeds remaining whole. The meal is sometimes eaten raw, the seeds being shaken out of it in the hand. More commonly, water is poured on the flour to extract the sugar and then drunk off. The dough that is left is carried to the mouth in handfuls, sucked out, and replaced, to be steeped a second time before being thrown away. Sometimes the fresh dough is patted into a huge jar-shaped cake, covered with wet sand, and baked. It comes out so hard that it has to be cracked with a stone."

[95] "The Mohave metate for corn, wheat, and beans is a rectangular block of lava on which a cylindrical muller is rubbed back and forth." (*Ibid.*, 736.)

Squashes which is common method of cooking them, the take a plug from the side extract the seeds from the hole and replace the Plug by which means they may roast them as neatly as if they were entire.

I found in this vicinity no beaver worth trapping for but remained here for the purposes of recruiting my men and horses. From the Indians I ascertained that below the rocky hills that came into the river and nearly down to the mouth of the Gila the country was barren and not inhabited. they also told me that it was about ten days travel to the spanish settlements in California. I swaped my poorest horses with the indians and endeavored to purchase others but without success.* (*One morning an Indian came to me and said the Indians had killed one of my horses which on examination I found to be true. They had killed the horse to eat and took away every thing but the entrails. from this time I had my horses so carefully guarded that they had no chance to continue their depredations.) Believing it impossible to return to the deposit at this season and in my present situation I determined to prepare myself as well possible and push forward to California where I supposed I might procure such supplies as woul[d] enable me to move on north.[96] In that direction I expected to find beaver and in all probability some considerable river heading up in the vicinity of the

[96] This passage seems to bolster Smith's later insistence on the fact that it was not his original intention to go all the way to California, but that it became expedient to do so at this point in his travels.

Great Salt Lake [97]   By this route I could return to the deposite. In pursuance of my plan I endeavored by all means in my power to procure a guide but could not succeed. I therefore got the best instruction I could in regard to the route and collected a supply of Corn, Beans, Locust Bread, and a little Indian flour.

Having remained at this place about 8 days I made a raft and crossed the river and for the first day traveled nearly west passing through the Rocky hills by a deep ravine which brought me through to the plain then a little north of west 15 miles to another range of hills where I found water and cane grass and encamped.[98] At night the most valuable horse I had was stolen for although I had a guard yet it was so dark that the horse was led out unperceived. The next day I travelled west

---

[97] The ever-elusive and legendary Buenaventura River, which figured so prominently in the hopes of many early explorers in the West. For more on the stream and its place in western lore, *see* C. Gregory Crampton and Gloria G. Griffen [Cline], "The Buenaventura, Mythical River of the West," 163-71.

[98] Smith left the Colorado at a point opposite of what was to become the site of Fort Mohave at about 35°03′ N. It was the departure point also used by Elliott Coues in 1865 as described in his *On the Trail of a Spanish Pioneer*, I, 235-6. The "Rocky hills" are the Dead Mountains which crossed Smith's path from north to south; the "deep Ravine" through which he traversed these mountains is one which begins at the N½, Sec. 5, T11N, R21E; and continues through the NE¼, Sec. 6, T11N, R21E and the SW¼, Sec. 31, T12N, R21E, of the San Bernardino Base Meridians. For this information and for an examination of the area, I am indebted to Mr. Todd Berens of Santa Ana, California, a remarkable teacher of a remarkable group of youngsters in the Explorer Club of Walker Junior High School, and in particular to Miss Loretta Yin who wrote the detailed report of the group's three-day field expedition to the area on Feb. 17-19, 1972. Smith's place of encampment was the present Piute Spring, a common first-day stopping point west of the Colorado.

through the range of hills to the plain where the trail could not be followed and where I was obliged to encamp without water.[99] I had supposed that I should be able to follow the trail from the directions given by the indians which being found impracticable and a great scarcity of water becoming more apparent I rode and sent others to the high hills and deep ravines in every direction to Look for water and as none could be found the Idea came forcibly to mind that it was the policy of the Indians to send me into the desert to perish.[100] In this situation I saw no alternative but to retrace my steps. on my way back I found an Indian and a boy following our trail for some purpose unknown to me. They had water with them which would convey the Idea that the country where I turned back was for some distance destitute of it. On seeing us one of them ran off I did not pursue him but kept the other with me until I got to the spring where I had before encamped.[101] It will be readily imagined that by this time we were much in want of water. During the night the

---

[99] Smith crosses the Piute Range and then, apparently in an effort to find the traditional Indian trail to San Gabriel, turns to the west and southwest and becomes lost in the lower Lanfair Valley in the general area of the Vontrigger Hills. His party was hoping to fall in with a route approximating that used by Francisco Garcés in 1776 which here ran along the southern end of Lanfair Valley, but more on this later.

[100] When Smith passed this way in Aug., 1827, on his next expedition, the Indians openly attacked, killing ten men among whom were Robeseau and Gobel of this party. Thomas Virgin, also a member of the present group was badly injured (Morgan, *Smith,* 240).

[101] That is, Piute Spring.

Indians ran off. The next day I moved to the river and found that the Indians had all gone from their Loges leaving everything the could not carry off.

It was now prudent to prepare for the worst which I did by making a pen for my horses and encamping under a bank of the River which would answer as a breastwork in the emergency which the singular conduct of the indians led me to expect. However the little renegade Francisco [102] (that spoke spanish) came to the opposite bank of the river in the morning and after hallowing plunged in and swam over. I asked the reason of the singular behaviour of the Indians. He said the Indians that got away from me told them I was coming back to kill them all for stealing my horse. To this I answered that it was all folly to tell them to return and be friendly as usual. It was true I must have my horse but I would not think of punishing the whole of them for the fault of the single scoundrel that stole him. I also told him to tell the chiefs that they must get the horse and bring him to me in which event all would be well. Francisco left me and in the evening the Indians returned to their Lodges. The chiefs came to see me and said that the Indian that stole my horse had gone off some distance but that they would have him back as soon as possible and oblige him to deliver the horse. They wished me to recross the river and as the grass

---

[102] Francisco, like the two Indians Smith ultimately engaged as guides for his trip across the Mojave Desert, must have been a runaway from Mission San Gabriel or one of its farms.

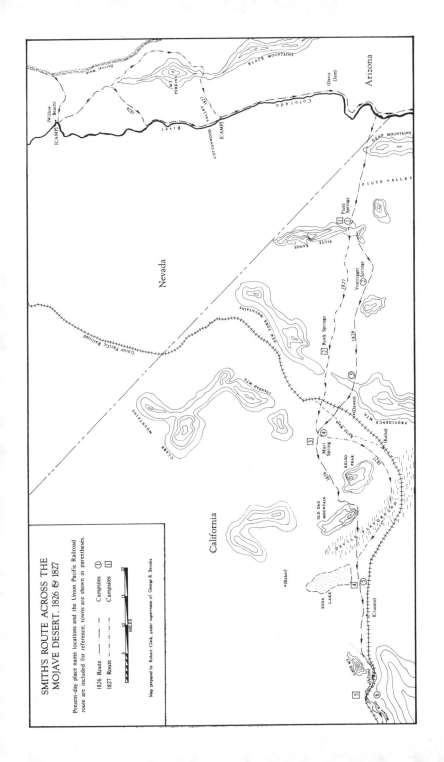

SMITH'S ROUTE ACROSS THE
MOJAVE DESERT, 1826 & 1827

Present-day place name locations and the Union Pacific Railroad
route are included for reference; towns are shown in parentheses.

1826 Route —··—··—   Campsites ⊕
1827 Route —···—···—   Campsites ☐

MILES
5   0   5   10   15   20

Map prepared by Robert Clark, under supervision of George R. Brooks.

Nevada

Arizona

California

Union Pacific Railroad

Colorado

BLACK MOUNTAINS

(Willow Beach)
[CAMP]

MT. PERKINS

DETRITAL WASH

1826

1827

ELDORADO VALLEY

(Davis Dam)

COTTONWOOD
[CAMP]

DEAD MOUNTAINS

PIUTE VALLEY

Piute Springs
☐ ⊕

PIUTE RANGE

Vontigger Springs ⊕

1827

1826

2 Rock Springs

NEW YORK MOUNTAINS

IVANPAH MTS

CLARK MOUNTAINS

3 Marl Spring
4 (Dawes)

5 KELSO MTS
(Kelso)

1826

PROVIDENCE MTS

KELSO PEAK

OLD DAD MOUNTAIN

1827

DEVILS PLAYGROUND

SODA LAKE

*(Baker)

(Crucero)

4

MOJAVE RIVER

(Afton)

5 6 CAVE MTS

was poor at that place I complied with their request and after crossing moved down the river about ten miles where the settlement is also considerable[103] and the country like that above with the exceptions that there are some small prairaes of tolerable good sandy soil producing Melons and corn and some ponds and slous in which portions of the river run in high water.[104] The grass at this place was much better than at any place above and the productions the same as those mentioned before though perhaps in greater abundance than in the upper part of the settlement. Their wheat is planted in hills. As they have no fences what few horses they have are kept constantly tied by a long halter and at this season are fed on Pumpkins and melons of which they appear verry fond. They ride without saddle or Bridle but by the help of a wide Circingle under which the slip their feet they are enabled to sit firmly. Melons were supplied in such numbers that I had frequently 3 or 400 piled up before my tent. A great many women and children were generally about us. Among the Amuchabas I did not find any verry influential chiefs.[105]

---

[103] Smith now moves farther down the Colorado River into the heart of the Mohave Valley – closer to present Needles, California – where the majority of the Indians lived.

[104] With little rainfall, and possessing no irrigation system, the Mohaves depended upon the annual spring floods of the Colorado to overflow the bottoms, create sloughs during the recession, and leave an alluvial deposit of moist mud in which they could farm (Kroeber, 735).

[105] The Mohaves had a class system with hereditary chiefs in the male line, but "they counted for little it would seem" (*Ibid.*, 741). Both Whipple, 113-18, and Ives, 67, mention meeting all or most of the five principal chiefs of the Mohaves during their visits.

He that has the most wives and consequently the most numerous connexion is the greatest man. There was one chief which we called Red Shirt from the circumstance of his wearing a shirt made out of a piece of red cloth which I had given him.[106] He was about 40 years of age and appeared to be a great favorite among the women. He frequently stayed at my tent and slept with any of the women he chose. No indians I have seen pay so much deference to the women as these.[107] Among indians in general they have not the privilege of speaking on a subject of any moment but here they harangue the Multitude the same as the men. While here Francisco came to me and requested I would go and see a man who was verry sick. I told him I was no Physician but these indians thinking a white man could do anything I was obliged to go to satisfy them. When I arrived at the spot 3 or 400 people were assembled but the man was dead. Seeing a large pile of wood I enquired of the interpreter the meaning he informed they were about to burn the corpse which was soon brought and laid on the pile, and also a small bag of net work containing his property. It appeared the man had died

---

[106] "Red Shirt" cannot be further identified. Red cloth, as Whipple and Ives also remark, was a desired gift, and red was apparently the Mohaves' favorite color. One of the reasons that the *Explorer,* Ives's curious little steamboat, attracted such attention was that "It [was] painted red, their favorite color . . ." (Ives, 66.)

[107] "The Mohave are at least as loose as any California Indians, and far franker about sexual relations. Marriage is living together at will . . ." (Kroeber, 747.)

from the swelled neck a disorder I think quite common
here as I observe many with their necks much scarified
a remedy which appeared to have been applied to the
case of the deceased as there was a good deal of Blood
on his neck. Two or three women were crying and
screaming and came to the pile apparently in the greatest agony embracing the corpse. They were pulled off
and fire was put to the pile which was soon in flames.
The mourners took some strips of Red cloth and whatever they thought most valuable and threw them in the
flames.[108] I left them but Francisco told me the deceased had two horses which were already killed and
on them the people would now feast. It being a great
object with me to procure a guide no means were left
untried and finally I succeeded in engaging two Indians
that lived in the vicinity of the Spanish Settlements.[109]
The stolen horse having been returned I moved to the
proper point and crossed over the River for the purpose
of making another attempt to cross the plain to California. Having remained at the Amuchabas several
days. The first day I traveled the same course as on the
preceeding attempt and encamped at the same spring.[110]

---

108 Mohave cremations were accompanied by a great deal of wailing and
mournful singing: "While the pyre is blazing, the shouts and lamentations are
at their height, property is thrown into the flames, and people even strip themselves of their garments." (*Ibid.,* 750.)

109 These two were imprisoned as runaways when they reached San
Gabriel, as Smith later reports under his entry for Nov. 30.

110 The Piute Spring, where Smith encamped on Nov. 10. In order to establish an itinerary for Smith's crossing of this portion of the Mojave Desert, it

The next day on the same route till I came to the place where I had before lost the trail then traveling a little north of west and passing some detached hills on the right and left Just before night we came to a hill of rocks and at its foot a small spring where I encamped.[111]

will be necessary to consider what he wrote about the route taken during his second transit. In 1827, with few supplies and fleeing hostile Indians who had just massacred ten of his party, Smith took off almost directly west, taking a path that in later years would be used by Lieutenant Whipple and become known as the Government Road.

"The Indians did not press us again," Smith wrote of his 1827 trip, "and just before dark we commenced our Journey and traveled all night and the next morning got to the first spring." (All quotations from Sullivan, *Travels*, 31-32.) After this stop at Piute Spring, however, the paths of 1826 and 1827 diverge. Continuing with 1827, Smith traveled on during the next night, but "In a low plain and in the night when I could not see the distant and detached hills. I had no guide by which to travel and therefor lost my way." He found a spring for this second stop and mounting a nearby hill he "was enabled to determine that we were about five miles on the right of the trail and nearly opposite a place where I had found water when I passed before." Smith then continues, "We remained at the spring until nearly night, and then bearing the spring on the [1826] trail to the left, I struck directly for the next spring on the old route. . ." This brings the 1826 and 1827 trails back together at a point which is, as we shall see, Marl Spring, and establishes that the location of his intermediate camp in 1827 was Rock Spring.

Morgan and Wheat, *Smith's Maps*, 64-65 and 71-72, examine the problem of establishing Smith's route in some detail, and although generally leaning toward a route we shall propose, had Smith starting from the Colorado at a point farther south, near Needles; they were also unaware of the number of camps his party made before reaching Marl Spring, and thus could not draw conclusive answers. Morgan, *Smith*, 415 n.14, suggests what proves to be the route Smith took in 1827 as the one he used the year previous, but this also must now be changed. The next few notes here, based on both the journal before us and what Smith said in his 1827 account, will hope to establish the correct itinerary for Smith's journey in 1826.

111 Instead of directly crossing through the middle of the Lanfair Valley as

In the vicinity was some gravelly hills on which there was a little grass where I turned my horses. The next day started early steering W N W crossing some ridges and passing some hills on our left. Just before night at the foot of a small hill we found a little spring or rather hole of water furnishing a verry inadequate supply for after taking out some to cook with I let the horses to it and they drank it all.[112] As there was no grass I was under the necessity of tieing my horses to keep them from running away. The next morning starting early a N W course about 1 O Clock I came to a little ravine in which was some grass and a spring here I en-

---

he will do in 1827, Smith moves to go along its southern perimeter. This time, with Indian guides, he was able, after crossing the Piute Range and moving southwest, to find the traditional Indian route and locate water at or near present Vontrigger Spring for his second camp (Nov. 11). This spring probably corresponds to that used on March 5, 1776, by Garcés (Coues, I, 236), whose route was what Whipple would later note as: "a wide prairie with an ascending slope, unobstructed by the mountains beyond. . . [which was] suposed to be the direct and ordinary route of the Indians to the vicinity of Los Angeles." (Whipple, 121.) That trail led northwest from present Sacramento Spring at Klinefelter into the north part of Fenner Valley toward Vontrigger Spring.

112 Smith's next stop is at a small spring somewhere in the Providence Mountains which cannot be exactly located. In traveling toward it, he keeps the Hackberry and Woods mountains on his left. Garcés, on his trip, also spent a night in the mountains ("a sierra that has pines, though small ones") at a spot Coues identifies as Cedar Springs (Coues, I, 236-37). Either this camp or the one previous would be about five miles south of Smith's 1827 route, but this seems the most likely candidate for the reference to "a place where I had found water when I passed before." Morgan and Wheat, *Smith's Maps*, 65, suggest that Smith's encampment was at a spring "high in the Providence Mountains near the Columbia Mine," but this does not seem to fit in with Smith's description of it being "at the foot of a small hill."

camped.[113] The country since leaving the Colorado has been a dry rocky sandy Barren desert. As my guides informed me that we had a hard days travel to make I moved off early keeping west down the ravine 5 miles Then S W and W S W till one O Clock when I came to border of a salt plain and at this place found some holes of Brackish water.[114] After crossing the Salt Plain I found a place where there was water and some grass and encamped.[115] The water was in holes dug about two

---

[113] Probably coming out of the Providence Mountains through Macedonia Canyon, Smith strikes northwest for the relatively short day's trek across Kelso Wash to Marl Spring. This was his fourth camp (Nov. 13) in 1826 but only his third stop on the more hurried trip the next year. The site was already known as Marl Spring when Whipple arrived in 1854; he found that "the spring was small, and there was not more than half enough water for the mules. But as it constantly though slowly flowed in, after awhile the animals were satisfied." (Whipple, 122.) Rogers daybook 1 lists two entries at "Ravine encampt." – a tin pan each to Martin McCoy and Abraham Laplant. Rogers gives the date of Oct. 13, but this, like his immediately preceding entry at the Mohave settlements is one month in error. Morgan and Wheat, *Smith Maps,* 65, using Rogers' date of the 13th, thought that the ravine encampment was the one in the Providence Mountains. It seems clear now, however, that Smith's and Rogers' "ravine" is the same one: Marl Spring.

[114] At this spot, on his second trip, the tired and thirsty Smith was gratified to relocate the water: ". . . it seemed a happy Providence that lead us to the little spring in the edge of the Salt Plain, for there was nothing to denote its place and the old trail was filled up with the drifting sand." (Sullivan, *Travels,* 33.) The spring must have been somewhere in the Devil's Playground.

[115] Smith, on Nov. 14, was now at his fifth camp from the Colorado and on the southern boundaries of Soda Lake, the name now given to the sink of the Mojave River. On his second trip he found the holes left from his camp: "After dark we proceed[ed] on across the Salt Plain and stopt at the hole I had dug when I passed before. . ." (*Ibid.,* 33.) This site corresponds to the general area of Garcés's encampment of March 9, 1776, where he found grass at what he called the Arroyo "de los Maitres" (Coues, I, 238-39), and Whipple's camp 142 of Mar. 8, 1854 (Whipple, 123).

feet deep and quite brackish making some new holes I found the water some better The Salt Plain I had passed during the day was about 15 miles long and from four to six miles wide. entirely Level and destitute of vegetation. Presenting a surface of sand the most beautiful Salt was found in many places and within two or three inches of the surface. I ascertained that although the salt was found in a Layer it did not extend throughout the plain. In passing the plain pieces of the salt were frequently throw out by the feet of the horses. The Layer was about ¾ of an inch thick and when the sand was removed from it I found the salt pure white with a grain as fine as table salt.

The next day W S W 8 or 10 miles across a plain and entered the dry Bed of a River on each side high hills. Pursuing my course along the valley of this river 8 or 9 miles I encamped.[116] In the channel of the river I occasionally found water. It runs from west to east alternately running on the surface and disappearing entirely in the sands of its bed leaving them for miles entirely dry. near the place where I entered its Bed it seemed to finally lose itself in the plain.* (* It is perhaps reasonable to suppose that the Salt Plain has been formed by the waters of this river overflowing the level country in its freshets and in the dry season sinking in the sand

[116] Smith's party, having found the mouth of the Mojave, continues up the stream to the usual first stopping point beyond Soda Lake, near present Afton. Known to earlier travelers as "The Caves," the spot was visited by Garcés on Mar. 10, 1776 (Coues, I, 239-40), and was Whipple's camp 144 on Mar. 10, 1854 (Whipple, 125).

and Leaving a deposit of salt on the surface. The waters of the River at this place are sufficiently salt to justify this conclusion.) At this time my provision was nearly exhausted although I thought I had provided enough to last me 10 or 12 days. But men accustomed to living on meat and at the same time travelling hard will Eat a surprising quantity of corn and Beans which at this time constituted our principal subsistence. One of my guides said he knew where his people had a cache of some provision and the next day as I traveled on he went with one of the men to procure some at night they returned bringing something that resembled in appearance loaves of bread weighing each 8 or 10 pounds. It was so hard that an ax was required to break it and in taste resembled Sugar Candy.[117] It was no doubt sugar but in that imperfect form in which it is found among nations to which the art of granulation is unknown. On

---

117 Apparently these cakes were not the baked screw mesquite loaves, a staple of the Mohave diet, which Smith observed in the Colorado settlement. Lt. Robert S. Williamson, during the course of his work on the railroad surveys, reports cane here in Nov. 1853: "In the cañon we found cane growing, similar to that mentioned as found in Walker's Pass, and large quantities of it had been cut by the Indians." (Lt. Robert S. Williamson, "Report of Explorations in California for Railroad Routes, To Connect with the Routes near the 35th and 32D Parallel of North Latitude," *Pacific Railroad Surveys*, v, 33.) Of his earlier encounter with the cane, Williamson wrote: "[The Indians] seemed at this season of the year [August] to be principally employed in collecting a kind of bulrush or cane, upon the leaves of which is found a substance very like sugar, which to them is a not unimportant article of food. They cut the cane and spread it in the sun to dry, and afterwards, by threshing, separate the sugar from the leaf. The cane itself had no sweet taste." (*Ibid.*, 15.)

enquiry I found it was made from the cane grass which I have before spoken of on adams River and the same of which the Amuchabas make their arrows. For three days nothing material occurred   Our course was up the River which sometimes run in sight and then for miles disappeared in the sands.[118] In places I found grass and the Sugar Cane and in some places small Cotton wood. I also saw the tracks of horses that had been here during the summer. My guides Belonged to a tribe of indians residing in the vicinity called the wanyumas.[119] not numerous for this barren country could not support them. At this place was some sign of Antelope and Mt sheep Mr. Rogers killed an Antelope which tasted quite strong of wormwood. On the 4th night from the salt plain an Amuchaba indian that had come this far with me disappeared.[120] I suppose he had become tired of the journey and returned. My guides had expected to find their families here but were disappointed.

The next day still following the course of the River which had a strong current in places 20 yds in width and in others entirely disappeared in the sands. After a long days travel I arrived late at a wan yu ma Lodge. close by were 2 or three families of the same tribe. Here

[118] Thus Smith's name for the stream, the Inconstant River.

[119] The Vanyume, a small and poor relative of the Serranos, who were all but extinct by 1923 (Kroever, 614-15). They were the "Beñemé" Garcés met, and whose pitiful condition he describes (Coues, I, 239-40).

[120] Garcés also notes that one of his Mohave guides turned back at about this point.

I remained the following day and in the mean time was well treated by these indians. They gave us such food as they had consisting of a kind of mush made of acrons and pine nuts bread made of a small berry.[121] This bread in appearance was like corn bread but in taste much sweeter. As there were in the neighborhood a plenty of hares the Indians said they must give us a feast. Several went out for this purpose with a net 80 or 100 yards long. Arriving at a place where they knew them to be plenty the net was extended among the wormwood. then divided on each wing they moved in such direction as to force the frightened game to the net where they were taken while entangled in its meshes. Being out but a short time they brought in 2 or three doz a part of which they gave me. seeing some tracks of antelope Mr. Rogers and myself went out and killed 2. In this vicinity there are some groves of Cotton wood and in places Sugar Cane and grass. On the following day after making the indians some presents I moved on keeping a right hand fork my course nearly S W passing out at the head of this creek and over a ridge I entered a ravin running S W I proceeded down it nearly to where it entered some high hills which were apparently covered with pine. At this place I encamped.[122] In the course of

---

[121] By now Smith has ascended the Mojave to near present-day Victorville. It was in this vicinity that Garcés found a "rancheria of some 40 souls of the same Beñemé nation. . . In this rancheria they regaled me with hares, rabbits, and great abundance of acorn porridge. . ." (Coues, I, 243-44.)

[122] Smith and his party now continue up the West Fork of the Mojave down into Summit Valley where the group encamps in the vicinity of what

the days I passed hills covered with a scattering growth of Bastard Cedar and bushy Oak. Some antelopes were seen in the course of the day and the tracks of Bear and Black tailed Deer.

The next day following the valley of a creek alternately sinking and rising and passing through a range of Mt for 8 miles where I was obliged to travel in the bed of the creek as the hills on both sides which were thick covered with cedar came in close and rugged to the creek. About ten miles from camp I came out into a large valley having no timber except what was on the creeks coming from the Mountains.[123] Here we found a plenty of grass and what was still more pleasing we began to see track of Horses and Cattle and shortly after saw some fine herds of Cattle in many directions. As those sure evidences of Civilization passed in sight they awakened many emotions in my mind and some of them not the most pleasant. It would perhaps be supposed

became Las Flores Ranch near where the river leaves the mountains. This section of the text finally confirms what George and Helen Beattie, Dale Morgan, and others held, namely that Smith on this trip did not use the Cajon Pass, but stayed slightly to the east and ascended the San Bernardino Range through Sawpit Canyon, the more traditional Indian route, and also the one used by Garcés in 1776 (*see* George William Beattie and Helen Pruitt Beattie, *Heritage of the Valley*, 23-24; Morgan, *Smith*, 200-01; and Coues, I, 245-46). From Smith's statement about his crossing in 1827: ". . . instead of traveling south East around the bend of the stream I struck directly across the Plain Nearly SSW to the Gape of the Mountain," this 1826 route could be theorized, but until now definite proof has been lacking.

123 The route takes Smith's band up Sawpit Canyon and then down Devil's Canyon and in to the San Bernardino Valley amongst the tributary creeks of the Santa Ana River.

that after numerous hardships endured in a savage and inhospitable desert I should hail the herds that were passing before me in the valley as harbingers of better times. But they reminded me that I was approaching a country inhabited by Spaniards. A people whose distinguishing characteristic has ever been jealousy a people of different religion from mine and possessing a full share of that bigotry and disregard of the rights of a Protestant that has at times stained the Catholic Religon.

They might perhaps consider me a spy imprison me persecute me for the sake of religion or detain me in prison to the ruin of my business I knew such things had been and might be again. Yet confiding in the rectitude of my intentions I endeavored to convince myself that I should be able to make it appear to them that I had come to their country as the only means by which I could extricate myself from my own embarrassing situation and that so far from being a spy my only [wish] was to procure such supplies as would enable me to proceed to my own country.

When we left the Mts our course was W S W Close on the right was a range of Mts out of which poured several beautiful streams watering a fertile valley extending many miles on the left. Having traveled about 18 miled I encamped.[124] We had nothing to eat and know-

---

[124] In traveling west through the valley, Smith remains along its northern rim, thus missing the chain of several farms belonging to the Mission San

ing that it would take two days to reach the settlements I determined to help myself to one of the hundreds of fine cattle in view. In endeavoring to kill one I had to use all the precaution necessary in approaching Buffalo. Having succeeded I found the animal branded on the hip I therefore saved the skin to carry in to the owner. At this place I remained during the following day.[125]

Gabriel which were to the south; their cattle, however, he could admire. It is impossible to determine the site of this particular camp for the information provided is vague. Rogers, in his daybook, records Arthur Black got a butcher knife, and James Reed and John Gaiter (sic.) each a pair of mocassins, and Smith a black silk handkerchief here at what Rogers called the "Rock Creek Encampment" on Nov. 25. But this does not help in locating the site. One strong possibility, given the distance Smith mentions, is that "Rock Creek" may indicate the party had reached San Antonio Creek, known earlier in history as the stopping point of Juan Bautista de Anza's caravan in 1776 (*see* Beattie and Beattie, 120-21). Morgan and Wheat, *Smith's Maps,* incorrectly read the date at Rock Creek as Nov. 22, which led them to place Rogers' reference at a camp either on the West Fork of the Mojave or Sawpit Canyon. Nov. 25, however, clearly denotes some spot in the San Bernardino Valley. The party actually arrived at this camp on the 24th; Rogers' entry refers to the second day in camp mentioned next.

[125] Nov. 25, considering Smith's next statement that it took two days to reach the "farm house." From this date until the party again crosses the San Bernardino Mountains in late Jan., 1827, Smith's account cannot be read without careful reference to the journal entries in Harrison Rogers' daybook 1. Very clearly there is a close connection between the two texts, and one can only hypothesize that Smith, in the absence of his own field notes, reconstructed much of this present narrative after his memory was refreshed by reading the Rogers manuscript. Smith's own notes of the journey up to this point (now missing) were turned over to Governor José Maria Echeandia in San Diego for transmittal to Mexico City, and it may well be that Smith kept no journal of his own while in southern California to allay Mexican suspicions that he was a spy. Rogers in this period becomes indeed the secretary of the expedition, possibly on instruction from Smith although such a theory may be far-fetched. From the physical arrangement of Rogers daybook 1, it is apparent

Again moving onward in two days travel I arrived at a farm house.[126] The country through which we passed was strikingly contrasted with the Rocky and Sandy deserts through which we had so long been traveling. There we had passed many high mountains rocky and Barren Many plains whose sands drank up the waters of the river and spring where our need was the greatest. There sometimes a solitary Antelope Bounded by to vex our hunger and the stunted useless sedge grew as in mockery of the surrounding sterility. There for many days we had traveled weary hungry and thirsty drinking from springs that increased our thirst and looking in vain for a boundary of the interminable waste of sands. But now the scene was changed and whether it was its own real Beauty or the contrast with what we had seen it certainly seemed to us enchantment. Our

-----

that a portion relating to the expedition's travels prior to reaching the San Bernardino Valley is missing. Rogers' first full entry is for November 27 (at La Puente, as we shall see), but that section is preceded at the top of the page by another which commences in mid-sentence. Undoubtedly Rogers had been keeping a journal for some time, but was the missing section also sent to Mexico, or did it survive to be used later by Smith for this narrative and then disappear? We are content to be thankful for what remains.

126 Smith has brought his men to an extensive dependency of Mission San Gabriel, the Rancho de la Puente, whose farm buildings, described later in the text, were located about two Spanish leagues east of the mission. The property was sold by San Gabriel in 1842 (Father Zephyrin Engelhardt, o.f.m., *San Gabriel Mission and the Beginnings of Los Angeles*, 202) and ultimately became the 48,000 acre grant awarded John Rowland and William Workman in 1845. Rogers daybook I gives Smith's date of arrival as Nov. 27. The party also stopped at La Puente on its first night after leaving San Gabriel for the return on Jan. 18, 1827.

path was through a fertile and well watered valley and the herds of Cattle and the bands of wild horses as they sniffed the wind and rushed wildly across our way reminded me of the Plains of the Buffalo East of the mountains that seemed to me as a home or of the cattle of the more distant prairaes of Missouri and Illinois.

Even in the Idea that we were approaching the abode of comparative civilization there was a pleasure not however entirely unmixed with dred for we knew not how we might be received. As we advanced the white Brant and Mallard were seen in great numbers it being now their season. and we passed a farm on a creek where a number of indians were at work. They gazed and gazed again considering us no doubt as strange objects in which they were not much in error. When it is considered that they were not accustomed to see white men walking with horses packed as mine were with Furs Traps Saddlebags Guns and Blankets and every thing so different from any thing they had ever seen and add to this our ragged and miserable appearance I should not have been surprised if they had run off at first sight for I have often been treated in that manner by savages. Arrived at the farm houses I was kindly received by an elderly man an indian who spoke spanish and immediately asked me if I would have a Bullock killed. I answered that I would and away rode two young Indians in a moment It being the custom in this country as I have since learned to keep a horse or horses constantly tied at the door Saddled and Bridled and of course ready to mount at a moments warning. In a short time the indians returned bringing a cow as fast as she could gallop. She was held between the two horsemen by ropes thrown over her horns and having the other end fast to the Pomel of the spanish Saddle one riding before and the other behind she was forced along without the power of resistance. They were anxious that I should shoot the cow which I did. Novel as the scenery of this country was to me It seemed that we ourselves were a still greater wonder to our semi-civilized friends. As I afterwards learned they wondered how indians could be so white having no Idea that civilized people lived in the direction from which we came. It was also a great wonder to them that we had guns and other articles and more than all that there should be with us one of the people of Reason this being the name by which they were learned to distinguish Spaniards from indians and which they readily applied to one of my men who spoke spanish.[127]

The farm house consisted of Two Buildings each about 100 feet long 20 feet wide and 12 feet high placed so as to form two sides of a square.[128] The walls are of unburnt brick about 2 feet thick and at intervals of 15

---

[127] Most likely it was Abraham Laplant who was accepted by the Indian neophytes as one of the *gente de razon* (*see* note 85).

[128] Rogers (daybook 1 entry for Nov. 27) was reminded of a "British Barracks" by the arrangement of the buildings at La Puente. Dale, 190, mistakenly interpreted the remark as a reference to San Gabriel itself.

feet Loop holes are left for the admission of light. The roofs were Thatched. It should be premised that I had at this time but a vague idea of the peculiarities of the country in which my fortune had placed me. I therefore was in the dark as to the manner in which I should conduct myself and determined to be guided by circumstances as they should transpire. In pursuance of this plan when the old overseer asked me if I was not going to write to Father [129] I told him I was and immediately set down and wrote a few lines briefly stating where I was from and the reason of my being there an Indian mounting one of the horses that are always in readiness took my note and was off in an instant. In about an hour the answer was returned by a man who the overseer told me was the commandant but in fact a Corporal.[130] He asked me how I did and congratulated me that I had escaped the Gentiles and got into a christian country and offering me some Segars made with paper according to the common custom of the country when I would take one he insisted that I should take the bunch. He then presented the note from the Father written in Latin and as I could not read his Latin nor he my english it seemed that we were not likely to become general correspondents. I however

[129] Father José Bernardo Sánchez (1778-1833), the amiable Franciscan about whom so much has been written, had become head of Mission San Gabriel earlier in 1826 (Engelhardt, 143). Rogers daybook 1 contains many flattering references to Fr. Sánchez as does the present text.

[130] Most of the missions had a corporal's guard in residence for security against any possible Indian trouble.

ascertained that he wished me to ride to the Mission so giving Mr. Rogers instructions how to proceed in my absence I took my interpreter and in Company with the corporal and a soldier moved on at the gate that appears quite common in this country a gallop passing large fields laid out on both sides of the road and fenced with Posts set in the ground with rails tied to them by means of strong pieces of raw hide there being also thousands of Cattle skulls in rows on each side of the road conveying the Idea that we were approaching an immense slaughter yard. Arrived in view of a Building of ancient and Castle-like appearance[131] and not knowing why I was brought there or who I was to see the current of my thoughts ran so rapidly through my mind as to deprive me of the power of coming to any conclusion so that when we passed in front of the Building and the Corporal after pointing to an old man sitting in the portico and observing that there was the father immediately rode off   I was left quite embarrassed hardly knowing how to introduce myself. Observing this I presume the father took me by hand and quite familiarly asked me to walk in making at the same time many enquiries.[132] Soon some bread and cheese were brought

---

[131] Thus Smith arrives at San Gabriel, then one of the richest and most prosperous of the California missions.

[132] Alfred Robinson, in his anonymously published recollections of life in California, described Fr. Sánchez as "possessing a kind, generous, and lively disposition," and continues that "he had acquired in consequence, a multitude of friends, who constantly flocked around him; whilst through his liberality the needy wanderer, of whatever nation or creed, found a home and protec-

in and some rum of which I drank to please the Father but much against my own taste. I then related to him as well as in my power the course of my being in that country but it was being to him a thing so entirely new and my interpreter perhaps not giving a correct translation of my words he was not able to comprehend the subject and told me there was an American residing in the vicinity for whom he would send as he spoke good Spanish and on his arrival we might have a good understanding.[133] In the mean time he told me to make myself as contented as possible and consider myself at home. He ordered the steward to show me to a room about 20 feet square in which there was a bed taking possession of it I was left alone to reflect on my singular situation for about two hours when the bell ringing for Supper a boy came and invited me in. The Old Father invited me to pass up next to him. We were seated on a long

---

tion in the Mission." ("An American" [Alfred Robinson], *Life in California* [New York, 1846], 31.)

[133] This man will turn out to be Joseph Chapman, the first American to settle in Los Angeles. "Claiming to have been shanghaied in the Sandwich Islands, Chapman was a member of the coast-raiding party of Hypolyte Bouchard, which sacked and burned Monterey in 1818. Chapman and two sailors went ashore from the *Santa Rosa* and were arrested. Chapman was taken to Southern California, where the missionary priests soon discovered that the prisoner knew how to build a grist mill, how to fell a tree, construct a schooner, splint broken bones, boss a gang of Indians, pull teeth, fashion farm implements, and make soap. When he arrived in San Gabriel in 1821 to build a grist mill . . . he became the favorite of Father Sánchez. The friar marveled that this strong young man, who had been so long 'in the darkness of Baptist faith' could give such an example of true piety to older Christians." (William W. Robinson, *Los Angeles from the Days of the Pueblo*, 30.)

bench with a back to it one of these occupying each side of the table. On The opposite side of the table sat a Spanish Gentlemen and a father from the neighboring village of the Angels [134] and the steward of the mission. at my side sat my interpreter. As soon as we were seated the Father said Benediction and each one in the most hurried manner asked the blessing of heaven – and even while the last words were pronouncing the fathers were reaching for the different dishes. About a doz Indian boys were in attendance who passing the different dishes to the fathers they helping themselves and passing them to the next. Our knives and forks according to the common custom of the country were rolled up in a napkin and laid by the side of the plates. The supper consisted principally of meats. and an abundance of wine. Before the cloth was removed Cigars were passed around. I may be excused for being this particular in this table scene when it is recollected that It was a long time sinc I had had the pleasure of sitting at a table and never before in such company.

---

[134] The Spanish gentleman is probably Francisco Avila, a prominent resident of Los Angeles who had been *alcalde* there in 1810. Smith calls Avila his friend later in the text, and it may be this meeting on Smith's first day at San Gabriel that began their association.

The priest might well be Fr. Gerónimo Boscana. The church of Nuestra Senora de Los Angeles (today's Plaza church), although dedicated on Dec. 8, 1822, functioned more as an *assistencia* of San Gabriel than as a parish in itself (Engelhardt, 136-37; and Maynard Geiger, O.F.M., *Franciscan Missionaries in Hispanic California*, 29-32). Fr. Boscana cared for the church from May 18, 1826, to June 27, 1831, according to The Rev. Francis J. Weber, Chancery Archivist in Los Angeles, whose book, *Catholic Footprints in California*, 132-33, contains a biographical sketch of the priest.

November 28th 1826 [135] My party arrived and I had my things put into the room which I occupied. The Corporal who was called Commandant came to me and after a few preparatory compliments observed that the best thing I could do with my guns would be to put them in his charge where they would be safe for said he strangers visiting you will be constantly handling them they being a kind with which they are unacquainted. I thanked him for his kindness and gave him the arms though I knew he was influenced by a motive verry different from the one assigned.

29th Just at sunrise Mr Rogers and myself were sent for showed forward to the table and served with tea Bread and Cheese. The father was not present for at that time he was at his devotions. It may perhaps be well for me in this place to give a view of some facts that were in part learned after this time anticipating my story that my ideas may be the more readily understood. California was first settled by missionaries of the order of St. Francis about 60 years since. These missions are scattered over the country and include in their several jurisdictions nearly all the natives of the country. The number of indians attached to each mission varies from 400 to 2000. These establishments with their dependencies include about ¾ths of the Inhabitants of California. The place at which I was for the time located

---

[135] From this date until Smith departs for San Diego, the reader should compare Smith's account with entries for the same dates in the Rogers daybook. The connection between the two will become evident at once.

was the mission of St Gabriel. The situation of St. Gabriel is pleasant the prospect to the North embracing a considerable range of Mts at the distance of 12 miles: on the south low hills:[136] and on the East and west a smooth country covered with grass. The soil in the vicinity of the mission has the appearance of great fertility presenting a gentle slope to the south East. The hills produce Pine of different kinds and at their feet Groves of Low Oak and small walnuts. The Streams are skirted with Cotton wood Ash willow small Buck Eye and wild Grape vines. Two thousand acres of land fenced in the manner I have before described and so situated as to be easily watered by a small creek that runs through it producing an abundance of Wheat Beans Peas and some Corn. An extensive vineyard and orchards of Apples Peach Pear and Olive trees some figs and a Beautiful grove of about 400 Orange trees render the Mission of St Gabriel a scene on which the eye cannot fail to rest with pleasure. On the beautiful lands of the neighborhood are grazing immense herds of Cattle and large bands of Horses. The buildings of the mission form a Hollow square. The Church on the S E and the Guard House on the S W corner the several sides being occupied by the Fathers Rooms office dinning Room apartments for Strangers. Store Houses Granaries Soap Factory Distillery Black Smith Carpenters and Cooper Shops The Shops for the Manufac-

---

[136] The mountain ranges are the San Gabriel to the north, and the Santa Ana on the south.

ture of Blankets and Lodging rooms for the unmarried women. at a short distance from the square the intermediate space being unfenced there is a street lined with small buildings on both sides these are occupied by the Indians of the Mission who have families.[137] At 11 O Clock the Father came and invited us to dinner. We accompanied him to the office adjoining the dining room and after taking a glass of Gin and some bread and cheese we seated ourselves at the table which was furnished with Mutton Beef Chickens Potatoes Beans and Peas cooked in different ways. Wine in abundance made our reverend fathers appeared to me quite merry. an express had been forwarded by the Commandant to the Governor at San Diego.*[138] (*My two indian guides were put in prison immediately on my arrival charged with being runaways from the Mission. They were about 16 years of age and from what I saw of them I thought them fine honest and well disposed boys.[139])

[137] Fr. Engelhardt's monograph on San Gabriel is the best source for the history of the mission. For a description roughly contemporary with Smith's, the reader is referred to "An American," 31-34; or to Fr. Sánchez's own inventory of the mission's lands, dated Dec. 5, 1827, in Engelhardt, 141-43.

[138] The Governor, of whom more later, was Don José Maria Echeandia.

[139] Rogers, in his daybook entry for Dec. 10, tells of a flogging at San Gabriel. A rather detailed description of the punishment administered to runaway neophytes was given by Fr. Estaban Tapis, president of the California mission in 1803. A portion is quoted in Richard F. Pourade, *Time of the Bells,* 110. Although sometimes severe, the punishment was handed down with a feeling of benevolence, for, as Fr. Tapis concluded: "Such are the chastisements which we inflict on the Indians in keeping with the judgment with which parents punish their own beloved children . . . For these chastisements generally the assistance of the *comandante* or of the guard is not solicited."

30th November   Sunday   A wedding at church but I did not attend being a protestant. I thought it might not be agreeable to the Catholics. the new married couple dined with us the bride and her sister being the only females present two or three young men attended with the groom. Mr Rogers and myself in our unfashionable dress would have verry willingly absented ourselves but no excuses would be received. Our dinner consisted of more than the usual number of dishes. Dried Grapes were served as a desert a Dozen Indians were playing on violins and the soldiers were firing their Musquets at the door. After dinner I spoke to the Commandant for another room for my men which was readily provided. I also proposed that instead of furnishing my men with their provision ready cooked as had been the case heretofore they should receive the material and cook them to their own taste to this he assented but observed that they might as well as not have an Indian to assist them. Flour Meat Beans &c were provided in abundance.

From this time nothing material occurred for several days. Mr Chapman the american spoken of by the Father came from the village of the angels accompanied by Capt Anderson of the Brig Olive Branch [140]

---

[140] Should be Captain William Henderson. The error was probably made by the transcriber, as Smith correctly mentions Henderson later in this text when the captain vouches for him in San Diego. Rogers daybook I does not mention this visit by Chapman, Henderson and Scott.

and the supercargo Mr. Scott.[141] Mr Scott being a good translator I was enabled to make my situation fully known. I soon ascertained that nothing could be done until the arrival of an answer from the Governor at San Diego. Besides the above named Gentlemen there came to St Gabriel at different times two others who spoke good English John Baptiste Bonnifacio [142] a Portuguese residing at St Francisco and on his way to St. Diego the other Señor Martinas [143] a native of S America and formerly in good circumstances. But being a Royalist lost his property and sought a retreat among the Fathers in California who are geny. secret friends of Ferdinand. Señor Martinas had lately been called to Mexico and was then on his way he appeared to be a man of science and business "You will find (says he.) it verry difficult

---

[141] James (sometimes "Diego") Scott, who also signed the testimonial in San Diego, was a Scotsman who settled in California. He died at Santa Barbara in 1851 (Hubert Howe Bancroft, *California Pioneer Register and Index, 1542-1848*, 322).

[142] Juan B. Bonifacio made his visit on Dec. 1 according to Rogers' daybook. Rogers calls him an "Itallian Gentlman, from Port Sandiego," and Bancroft thought him either Italian or Austrian (Bancroft, *Register*, 63). Bonifacio had landed in California from the *John Begg* in 1822 and was later naturalized. Dale's note on Bonifacio is based on Bancroft (Dale, 200 n.414).

[143] Francisco Martinez, noted by Rogers as a "Spanish Gentleman" was at San Gabriel on Dec. 7 and 8 according to the daybook. He apparently lost his property in the Mexican revolt in 1822 and was expelled under the law of 1827 along with other Spaniards (Bancroft, *Register*, 241; Dale, 200, n.418). Dale's note here is in error, for it is made in reference to "Mr. Francisco the spanish Gentleman that he [Smith] went to visit" at Los Angeles, who is Francisco Avila. "Francis Martinnis" appears in the Rogers daybook 1 entry for Dec. 7, and "Martina" on Dec. 8.

to make the Governor Comprehend your business. He has been raised without knowing the hand that fed him as a Gentlemen and those Mexican Gentlemen know verry little of business of any kind and much less of yours. He may perhaps detain you here a long time he will not consider the expense of the wages of your men nor your anxiety to join your partners.

Improving the opportunity offered by my presence I learned from Father Sanchez that at the different farms belonging to the Mission (St Gabriel) there were 40,000 head of Cattle 2,000 horses 3 or 400 head of Sheep and a great many hogs of these last the make little use.[144] There are but few white men at this place neither could it be expected there would be many in California for father Sanchez told me that no white woman had ever come there to live. There are attached to the Mission of St Gabriel about   [145] Indian Inhabitants who are kept in the strictest order being punished severly for the most trifling offence or neglect.

---

[144] Smith's inventory is somewhat at variance with the one made by Fr. Sánchez on Dec. 5, 1827: "The number of cattle which the Mission possesses, according to the reports it annually transmits to the government, will reach more or less 18,400 head: of horses, 2,400 in all; of mules, 130; of sheep, 14,000; of pigs, 150; of goats, 50 . . ." (Engelhardt, 141).

[145] The transcriber had left a blank for later insertion of the number. A *padrón,* or list of Indians belonging to the mission, besides the rancherias, gave 2,502 as having been confirmed on Jan. 1, 1824 (*Ibid.,* 144). Rogers (daybook entry for Nov. 29) estimates the total Indian population at San Gabriel at upwards of 1,000. James O. Pattie, for what his figures are worth, claims to have vaccinated 960 individuals at San Gabriel in March 1829, and 2,500 at Los Angeles – which then had a population of under 1,000 (*Ibid.,* 155-56).

They are whipped like slaves the whip being used by an indian a soldier standing by with a sword to see that it is faithfully done. Having passed the age of puberty the two sexes if unmarried are kept separate being at night shut up in different apartments [146] the work of the day having their tasks [147] the ringing of the Bells in the morning which is quite early all the indians go to church and after prayers the overseers of the various branches of work receive their orders from the Principal Overseer and move off immediately to their several employments. An old man from the Angel village being at the mission invited me to visit him at his house and two or three days after sent his son with horses. I went taking with me my interpreter and was verry kindly received by my friend Francisco Abela.[148] The Angel village in which my friend resided contained 70 or 80 Houses The walls of mud or unburnt Brick and the roofs of thatch or tile. They were general small and few of them cleaner than they should be. This village is about ten miles S W from St. Gabriel the inhabitants cultivate but little ground depending on their Cattle for subsistance. They are generally poor

---

[146] Loss occasioned by hole in manuscript.

[147] Loss occasioned by hole in manuscript.

[148] Rogers, in his entries for Dec. 1 and 2, tells of Smith – and Laplant – going to Los Angeles as a result of an invitaiton apparently extended by the gentleman (Francisco Avila) Smith mentions earlier in this text. Rogers says the man sent his servant, Smith says his son, to guide the two Americans. In any event, we can now state that Smith spent the night of Dec. 1, 1826 and another later on, in the Avila house at Los Angeles, a distinction not previously accorded this landmark.

but a few families are rich in Cattle horses and Mules and among these Señor Francisco Abela and his Brother Don Ignatio [149] are perhaps the richest. In California as in Spain the Siesta after dinner is fashionable. they generally sleep 2 or three hours. The Californians are excellent horsemen when on a swift horse they catch a wild steer or horse with the greatest ease. They are seldom seen on foot but mount a horse to go even 200 yards and always carry with them a strong rope made from pieces of Ox hide braided which is called a Larse. It is 7 or 8 fathoms in Length with a Loop at the end for the purpose of forming a noose. The Spaniard mounted on a swift horse with his Larse in hand holding it so as to form the noose about 4 feet in diameter and swinging it around his head to keep it connected pursues the wild Cattle and horses of that country and arriving at the proper distance while both pursued and pursuer are at utmost speed throws his noose with such precision as to generally succeed in fastening it to the animal in the intended place while at the same time with his left hand he takes a turn around the Pomel of the saddle which is made high for that purpose with the end of the rope remaining in his hand. If the animal pursued is a horse he is caught around the neck and is soon choked down. If a steer he is caught by the horns and generally by two persons one riding before the

---

[149] Antonio Ignacio Avila, who died in 1858 at the age of 74, and Francisco were two of the children of Cornelio Avila who settled in Los Angeles in 1783 (Bancroft, *Register*, 45).

animal and one behind holding him between them by their respective Larses with the power of resistance. If it is the object to throw the animal down they throw for the feet and having caught and fastened the rope to the saddle giving the horse a start the animals feet are taken from under him at once. In this manner they can take almost any animal in the country without excepting even the Elk but the principal use of this daring and active exercise is the catching of the wild horse and wild Cattle that range the country in great numbers. I am also informed that when a Bear can be found in the open country they are taken in this manner. But they do not attempt this adventure singly. Of the truth of this I have some doubts. The only Bear found in this country are the Grizly Bear smaller than those of the Mountains yet notwithstanding a formidable animal and possessing sufficient strength as I think to take hold of the Larse when noosed around the neck and tear it from the Saddle or break it in an instant.

8th December 1826   At this time the Mercury ranges from 50 to 70. Today the Corporal received orders to forward me to San Diego to pay a visit to his excellency Hosea Maria De Acheondia.[150] Capt Cunningham of the Ship Courier of Boston arrived about the same time from San Diego.[151]

---

[150] Governor Echeandia.

[151] Captain William H. Cunningham, a Bostonian, had been "trading on the coast for Hides and Tallow since June last," according to Rogers daybook I entry for Dec. 8. Dale, 203 n.421, has some additional biographical information. *See also* Bancroft, *Register,* 112.

9th December 1826   Capt Cunningham had been trading on this coast since the preceding July exchanging Dry goods Groceries and hardware for hide and Specie. The population not admiting of a wholesale business the sales are made in Retail while passing along the coast from Acapulco to St Francisco. At that time he expected to be on the coast about a year longer. He spoke Spanish and manifested the most friendly disposition and a willingness to render me all the assistance in his power. It was therefore with great pleasure that I learned he was about to return to San Diego and that we could travel in Company.[152] At 11 O Clock all preparations being made we started. My horses were furnished by government some being driven along for the purpose of having a change. A soldier was sent by the Commandant for a guide to take charge of the Loose horses and catch one if necessary. Just before starting the Comdt took care to tell me that he was instructed to send a good and careful Soldier. In this country horses are so plenty and cheap and the people have so little feeling for these noble animals (as I shall soon show) that they indulge freely in the common disposition for fast riding secure that when a horse is

---

[152] According to Rogers (daybook I entry for Dec. 9), Smith took with him "one of the men," a reference probably to Abraham Laplant who could act as interpreter. Morgan, *Smith,* 204, states that Smith took "the black boy, Peter Ranne as a servant," but we have already learned (note 9) that Ranne(y) was neither a black nor a servant, so this theory must be laid aside. There would have been no reason, otherwise, to take Ranney, who had no special skills Smith might need in San Diego.

no longer able to travel another may be cheaply and easily procured. We therefore fell in with the spirit of the time and people and moved off at a gallop over a fine level country. Four miles from St Gabriel we crossed a stream 50 yards wide and shallow and sandy.[153] On the right a country gently undulating extended to the Ocean a distance of 20 or 30 miles and on the left a range of high and rough hills.[154] About 18 miles from the first mentioned creek we crossed another 80 yards wide in appearance like the first and three miles further came to a farm.[155] In this distance we had passed many herds of cattle belonging to the residents of the Angel village and some thousands of wild horses.[156] The wild horses become so abundant at times as to eat the grass quite clean. My guide informed me that the inhabitants of the village and of the vicinity collect whenever they consider the country overstocked and build a large and strong pen with a small entrance and two wings extending from the entrance some distance to the right and left. Then mounting their swiftest horses they scour the country and surrounding large bands they drive them into the enclosure by hundreds. They will there perhaps

---

[153] The San Gabriel River.

[154] The Santa Ana Mountains.

[155] After crossing the second stream, the Santa Ana River, Smith and the party arrive at the Rancho de Santa Ana, an extensive property owned by Don Tomas Yorba.

[156] "The journey continued across a plain where thousands of cattle were grazing; and immense herds of wild horses, which fled swiftly to the mountains on our approach," was how Alfred Robinson viewed the same scene in 1829 ("An American," 31).

Larse a few of the handsomest and take them out of the pack. A horse selected in this manner is immediately thrown down and altered blindfolded saddled and haltered (for the Californians always commenc with the halter). The horse is then allowed to get up and a man is mounted. when he is firmly fixed in his seat and the halter in his hand an assistant takes off the blind the several men on horseback with handkerchiefs to frighten and some with whips to whip raise the yell and away they go. The poor horse having been so severely punished and frightened does not think of flouncing but dashes off at no slow rate for a trial of his speed. After running until he is exhausted and finding he cannot get rid of his enemies he gives up. He is then kept tied for 2 or 3 days saddled and rode occasionally and if he proves docile he is tied by the neck to a tame horse until he becomes attached to the company and then turned Loose. But if a horse from the moment he is taken from the pen proves refractory they do not trouble themselves with him long but release him from his bondage by thrusting a knife to his heart. Cruel as this fate may seem it is a mercy compared to that of the hundreds left in the pack for they are shut up to die a death most lingering and most horrible, enclosed within a narrow space without the possibility of escape and without a morsel to eat they gradually loose their strength and sink to the ground making at time vain efforts to regain their feet and when at last all powerful hunger has left them but the strength to raise their heads from the dust with which they are soon to mingle: their eyes that are becoming dim with the approach of death may catch a glimpse of green and wide spread pastures and winding streams while they are perishing from want. one by one they die and at length the last and most powerful sinks down among his companions to the plain. No man of feeling can think of such a scene without surprise indignation and pity. Pity for the noblest of animals dying from want in the midst of fertile fields. Indignation and surprise that men are so barbarous and unfeeling. A fact so disgraceful to the Californians was not credited from a single narrator but has since been corroborated.

But to return to this digression the farm of which I have before spoken belonged to Don Thomas (the remainder of his name I have forgotten).[157] he was not at home but his wife invited us into a house of 2 or three rooms and informed us that her husband was soon expected. we therefore concluded to wait his arrival. I observed some sugar cane growing in the garden which appeared quite thrifty. It was not long before

---

[157] Alfred Robinson enjoyed Yorba's hospitality in 1829 and described him as "a tall, lean personage, dressed in all the extravagance of his country's costume . . . Upon his head he wore a black silk handkerchief, the four-corners of which hung down his neck behind. An embroidered shirt, a cravat of white jaconet tastefully tied, a blue damask vest, short clothes of crimson velvet, a bright green cloth jacket with large silver buttons, and shoes of embroidered deer skin comprised his dress. I was afterwards informed . . . that on some occasions, such as some particular feast day or festival, his entire display often exceeded in value a thousand dollars." (*Ibid.*, 29-30.)

we were called to eat the attention of these people being in that respect truly proverbial. we sat down to a table where the Table cloth Napkins and plates were clean and the spoons of Silver but neither knives or forks were there for the common people of this country seldom have these articles. Our repast consisted of a hash highly seasoned with peper. Tortioes (pan cakes) and wine. The blessing was asked by a boy 8 or 9 years old standing at the end of the table with his hands raised. not being pronounced in the usual hurried manner it had much more the appearance of devotion   I then thought as now that some of the learned fathers might learn the air of devotion if not the substance from this little boy. Soon after we had finished eating Don Thomas arrived having ascertained our wants he said as his horses were some distance off we could have to remain all night or if we were in a great hurry we could start at one or two O Clock in the morning by which time he could have the horses. At two O Clock we started on our journey and at 8 O Clock arrived at the Mission of San Juan a distance of about 25 miles.[158] The first part of this distance being traveled in the night I could not so well form an Idea of its appearance. but it seemed much like that we had passed and judging from the noise the wild horses made in running when scared off by our approach or when taking the wind I would think them as numerous as in the country

---

[158] The Mission San Juan Capistrano.

before described. As we approached the Ocan the country became much more hilly. The Mission of San Juan
is about a mile from the Ocan in a country hilly and
barren. The buildings are similar in construction and
arrangement to those at St Gabriel. In the year 1811 the
church of this mission was nearly destroyed by an earthquake sinc which time service has been performed in
one of the smaller buildings.[159] The number of Indians
is not great at this Mission nor is it more than half as
rich as that of St Gabriel. On our arrival at San Juan
the people were at church as soon as service was over
the Steward invited us to take a cup of Chocolate which
is a beverage of which the Spaniards are verry fond
and of which the higher class make great use particularly in the morning. To Americans they generall offer
tea as they have an idea that we are verry fond of it.
I have seen them grind tea as they would coffee which
is an evidence that they do not make much use of it. My
soldier presented his instructions to the Corporal at the
Mission who soon supplied us with fresh horses and a
new Soldier. we then pushed on: our way leading us for
some miles directly along the beach of the Ocean.[160]
The country back rough and hilly. To an old an nearly
deserted Mission there being but an overseer and a few

[159] The earthquake actually occurred on Dec. 8, 1812. For an account of
the disaster *see* Zephyrin Engelhardt, o.f.m., *San Juan Capistrano Mission,*
53-55.

[160] Smith and his party were following the traditional route between the
missions, *El Camino Real.* Descending through the hills, the group travels
along the beach from San Juan Capistrano to present San Onofre.

indians to occupy it.[161] From this place our course was S E through hills covered with Bastard cedar till just at night when we arrived at the handsome Mission of San Louis Rey [162] a distance from St Juan I think about 50 miles. This Mission is beautifully situated on a rising piece of ground between two small creeks. The building were similar to those at San Gabriel but appeared better from having been lately whitewashed. On the East Side a Portico extended the whole Length of the buildings.

---

[161] There was, of course, no mission at San Onofre. Perhaps Smith refers here to some building of the Rancho San Mateo or the Rancho San Onófrio. An inventory of San Juan Capistrano's lands made in late 1827 puts both ranchos near Smith's position: "To the southeast, the Mission has the Rancho of San Mateo, distant three leagues, a little more or less. About half a league from the said rancho, the Mission of San Louis Rey has placed the Rancho of San Onófrio in the same direction. This occupies about three leagues of valley and hills; but all these lands which are good, belong to San Juan Capistrano, inasmuch as all the Indians of that district have been born there. Nevertheless, the said Mission of San Luis Rey has taken possession of that whole district. From what has been said, there remains the Rancho of San Mateo adjacent to the usurped lands and likewise to the Rancho of Las Flores of the Mission San Luis Rey." (Engelhardt, *San Juan Capistrano Mission*, 88-89.)

It is difficult to determine just what location Smith identifies here, but it is not the Rancho Las Flores, which having been established in 1823 would hardly have been "old an nearly deserted" when Smith passed. San Juan Capistrano apparently suffered substantially as a result of Echeandia's emancipation edict of July 25, 1826, and much of its property fell into disrepair after the Indians on the missions were "freed." (*Ibid.*, 80-82.)

From San Onofre, the party follows the established route up along the San Onofre River and moves on southeast, passing Las Flores on the way to San Luis Rey.

[162] Mission San Luis Rey was, at the time of Smith's visit, perhaps the most prosperous of the California missions and had considerable land holdings. Alfred Robinson was also very favorably impressed during a visit of a few days in 1829 ("An American," 23-26).

Remaining there during the night and in the morning making an exchange of soldiers and horses we proceeded on through a hilly country about 30 miles to San Diego.[163] When we arrived at the Presidio I was taken to the office of the Lieutenant and on the arrival of an interpreter procured by Capt Cunningham I was informed that I could not see the Gov until the next day. Presently Capt Dana [164] of the Ship Waverly from the Sandwich Islands came and invited me to his quarters. Having ascertained that I would be at Liberty to choose my residence I accompanied him to a private house about ¼ of a mile from the Presidio where Capt Cunningham and himself always put up when on shore. Capt Dana was a Bostonian and a verry friendly man.

---

[163] Alfred Robinson, who was making the trip from south to north, wrote of this part of the route: "We saw no habitations on the route, and the soil was one continual waste of bareness, entirely destitute of cultivation. A few scattered trees adorned the road, and now and then a deer was seen running over the hills, or a hare, or rabbit sat basking in the sun, among the low shrubbery. This, with the exception of a passing traveller, or a casual glance of the sea, was all that met the eye during a ride of forty miles. The great number of hills which it is necessary to surmount makes the way very tedious, and to the traveller they seem almost endless." (*Ibid.*, 23.) This section of the *Camino Real* took Smith south from San Luis Rey to what is now Del Mar and vicinity; then the road detoured inland up Soledad Valley and down Rose Canyon (the Santa Fe Railroad's right-of-way today), and skirted behind La Jolla and inland of Mission Bay to reach the Presidio San Diego. Smith's arrival date would be Dec. 11, 1826.

[164] Captain William Goodwin Dana, master of the brig *Waverly,* was naturalized and married to a young California girl in 1828. For a brief biographical sketch, *see* William Henry Ellison (ed.), "Recollections of Historical Events in California, by William A. Streeter," 175 n.40. *See also* Bancroft, *Register,* 114.

The following day I went to see the Gov or Genl (as he is known here by both of those titles although when at Mexico I am told he ranked as a Major).[165] When I let him know my situation and my wants he told me it would be some days before he could give me an answer as it would be necessary to call a Council of officers &c. In the mean time he observed I should be furnished with a Room and every necessary with such clòthing as I wanted for as I had on my leather Hunting shirt he readily supposed a change would be desirable. I thanked him for his kindness but told him as Capt Cunningham was my Countryman I would prefer remaining with him and being under obligations to him for any supplies I might want. He acquieseed and I accompanied Capt Cunningham on board his Ship Courier and was told to consider it my home. I there became acquainted with Mr Shaw the super cargo Mr Theodore Cunningham 1st mate a brother of the Capt and Mr Blackder 2d Mate.[166]

---

[165] Echeandia, a "tall, gaunt personage" (Alfred Robinson, 17), was "simply colonel of artillery; but as he had the title and authority of the commandant general, civil and military chief of the two Californias *(comandante general jefe politico y militar de ambas Californias),* he was given that of general in the country; and in addressing him, that of Your Lordship (Usia). He enjoyed the most extensive power, and he frequently made ill use of it." (Charles Franklin Carter, "Duhaut-Cilly's Account of California in the Years 1827-1828," 161). August Duhaut-Cilly devotes several paragraphs to comments about Echeandia.

[166] Thomas Shaw will appear again as one of those who signed the testimonial for Smith. "Blackder" should be "Blackler," but the Peabody Museum, Salem, Mass., which owns the log for this trip of the *Courier* has no information about him, not even his first name.

The Precidio * (* Precidio is a name applied to a town which is the residence of the Governor.) of San Diego is about three miles from the harbor in Latitude [167] The buildings are in a square somewhat like the Missions but lower and much decayed.[168] they are on a side hill sloping toward the Ocean. The residence of the Governor is on the East and his portico commands a fine view of the harbor and the Ocean. San Diego contains about 200 inhabitants exclusive of the Mission of the same name which is about 6 miles North East on a small stream [169] which flows into the harbor. The general aspect of the country is hilly and barren with some Scrubby Oak and Pine on the hills but verry little grass.

The harbor of San Diego is formed by two Peninsula's one of which projects into the Ocean directly oposite the Precidio. The entrance is quite narrow but having a great depth of water and being entirely protected from winds this harbor is considered very safe. A Block house or fort on the Peninsula commands the entrance of the harbor.[170]

---

[167] The transcriber has left a blank for the later insertion of a number.

[168] Smith was not alone in his opinion that things at San Diego were somewhat rundown. "Of all the places we had visited since our coming to California, excepting San Pedro, which is entirely deserted, the presidio at San Diego was the saddest. It is built on the slope of a barren hill, and has no regular form; it is a collection of houses whose appearance is made still more gloomy by the dark color of the bricks, roughly made, of which they are built. . . The fine appearance of [the mission] loses much on nearing it; because the buildings, though well arranged, are low and badly kept up. A disgusting slovenliness prevails in the padres' dwelling." (Carter, "Duhaut-Cilly," 218-19.)

[169] The San Diego River.

Several days having passed I called again on his Excellency but could get no answer. He told me he did not know what to do he must see my journal and he likewise took a copy of my chart and License.[171] He even asked me what business I had to make maps of their country. I told him my maps were made merely to assist me in traveling and must of necessity be verry incorrect as I was destitute of the means for making celestial observations – from this time I was detained day after day and week after week. Sometimes he told me I must wait until he could receive orders from Mexico and at other times he thought it desirable that I should go to Mexico and would then come to the conclusion that it was necessary to send myself and party to Mexico. Whilst my fate depended on the caprice of a man who appeared not to be certain of any thing or of the course his duty required him to pursue and only governed by the changing whims of the hour my feelings can only be duly appreciated by those who have been in the same situation. I knew the eager expectations with which my

---

[170] Fort Guijarros, on the neck of Ballast Point, was California's first coastal fortification. Plans for it were completed in 1795 and it was built during the next decade. The fort's one significant engagement was with the American trading vessel *Lelia Byrd* in 1803; the place was abandoned in 1838. (*See* the San Diego Federal Writers' Project, *San Diego, A California City,* 155, for details.)

[171] These were apparently sent on to the Minister of War in Mexico City, for the letter of transmittal, dated Dec. 30, 1826, is known. A digest is in Department State Papers, xxx, 37-38, Bancroft Lby., Berkeley, Calif. (Morgan, *Smith,* 416 n.24).

party at St Gabriel Looked for my return. I felt the ruinous effect which my detention had on my business and the gloomy apprehensions which my protracted absenc would cause to my partners in the distant Mountains. But these considerations never came within the sphere of his Excellency's comprehension and I was harrassed by numerous and contradictory expedient and ruinous delays until about the first of January when his Excellency informed me that if the Americans who were in the harbor of San Diego Masters of Vessels officers and Supercargo would sign a paper certifying that what I gave as the reason of my coming to that country they believed to be substantially correct I might then have permission to trade for such things as I wanted and to return the same route which I had come in.[172] I had applied for permission to travel directly north that I might arrive as soon as possible on the territory of the United States but this he would not grant Insisting that I should travel the same route by which I had come. The certificate was made out and signed by Capt Wm H. Cunningham Theodore Cunningham and Mr Shaw of the Ship Courier Capt Dana

---

[172] One wishes Smith had been more explicit in describing his situation and activities during his stay in San Diego. What he offers here really adds nothing to what was not already known from other sources. In fact, it contains less information, if one considers there is no mention of the letter Smith sent to Rogers about Dec. 16 (*Ibid.,* 205) requesting beaver skins be sent him to give to the officials at San Diego for facing their cloaks (Rogers daybook I, entries for Dec. 18, 19).

and Mr Robbins [173] of the Waverly Capt Henderson and Mr. Scottie of the Brig _____ belonging to Bags & Company of Lima.[174] The Governor then gave me a passport and License to purchase such supplies as I wanted. I was allowed the privilege of staying but 4 days after my arrival at St Gabriel and strictly forbid to make any more maps for said the Gov even our own Citizens can not make maps unless permission is obtained from Mexico. Although the Governor had obliged me to go to San Diego yet he would not furnish me with horses for my return. But I felt this injustice

---

[173] Thomas M. Robbins (not Robinson, as Dale, 209, would have us believe) came to California as mate on the *Rover* in 1823. At his death in 1857 he was "remembered as a hospitable, good-natured old salt" (Bancroft, *Register,* 305). *See also* Ellison, "Recollections," 174. Robbins was to become the brother-in-law of his captain, William G. Dana; both men married daughters of Don Carlos Carrillo – Dana wed Josefa in 1828, and Robbins wed Encarnacion in 1834. The document mentioned is in the Department State Papers, II, 19-21, at the Bancroft Lby. (Morgan, *Smith,* 416 n. 26), and is printed in Dale, 209 n.427.

[174] Henderson and Scott were on the *Olive Branch,* as Smith reported when he met them at San Gabriel shortly after his arrival. Why the brig's name is omitted here is not known. According to Bancroft, *History of California,* II, 148, the *Olive Branch* was consigned to Mancisidor of Callao, Peru. John Begg and Company of Glasgow and Lima, was the first commercial house to have connections in California and the principal factor in the hide and tallow trade on the Pacific coast. For an account of some of the firm's activities, *see* Adele Ogden, "Hides and Tallows, McCulloch, Hartnell and Company, 1822-1828," 254-64. Juan Ignacio Mancisidor and his partner, Stephen Anderson, were also active in the hide and tallow trade, and probably hired the brig from Begg and Company.

James Scott, incidentally, had become settled enough in his California ways to sign himself "Diego" on this particular document.

the less as Capt Cunningham offered me a passage on board of his ship which would sail in a few days for point Pedro the nearest Anchorage to St Gabriel. I accepted this offer the more readily as it would enable me to have my supplies prepared during the passage for they were to be procured from Capt Cunningham. I had found the Governor to more than sustain the character given of him by Señor Martinas and it will be readily supposed that I left him without any other regret than what I felt for the time lost in doing business that might have been done in a few hours or might as well have been left undone. Every thing being ready we sailed and on the third day came to anchor on the East side of the Island of St Catalina.[175] The Island of Santa Catalina is about 20 W S W from St Pedro. It is about 18 miles long and 8 broad having high hills covered with grass wild onions and some small timber. Capt Cunningham had a house on the Island for the purpose of salting hides.[176] He was about to take some Cows Hogs and fowls for the use of the men there employed. after remaining at the Island 2 nights we sailed for St Pedro which is merely a good anchorage

[175] The log of the *Courier,* which unfortunately contains no reference to Smith, reveals that the brig sailed from San Diego on Jan. 5, 1827, and anchored off Santa Catalina on Jan. 8, the third day out from the mainland. *See* Capt. William H. Cunningham, *Log of the Courier, 1826-1827-1828.*

[176] For a detailed and graphic explanation of drying hides and all other aspects of the California trade, there is no finer account than that found in Richard Henry Dana, Jr.'s, *Two Years Before the Mast.*

or road stead.[177] several Cannon were fired as a Signal to a farmer that lived 8 or 10 Miles off who usually made it his business to come with horses to take people up to the Pueblo or to St Gabriel. As the expected horses did not come we started on foot and continued until we procured horses to take us to the Pueblo los Angelos or the Angels Village. We remained all night at the village and in the morning I called on my friend Señor Abella and made arrangements for the purchase of horses and then in Company with the Capt Mr. Chapman and Mr. Shaw I moved on to the Mission of St. Gabriel where I found my party all well.[178] I must not omit the cordial welcome with which I was received by father Jose Sanches. He seemed to rejoice in my good fortune and well sustained the favorable opinion I had formed of him. You are now (says he) to pass

---

[177] The *Courier* log mentions landing cattle on Jan. 8, and then setting sail for San Pedro at 5:00 p.m. that same day, if one interprets the Jan. 9 entry as beginning on the preceding evening: "TUESDAY 9TH. Commences with moderate breeze and pleasant weather. At 5 p.m. got under weigh and made sail for St. Pedro . . . At 3:30 a.m. moderate made all sail wind S. Easterly. At 11:30 anchored off the Pt. of St. Pedro . . ." This entry must refer to the night of Jan. 8-9, with an arrival at San Pedro on the morning of the 9th. Such an interpretation, along with Smith's mention of an overnight stay with Francisco Avila, would put him back at San Gabriel on the Jan. 10 date given in Rogers daybook I. This itinerary conflicts somewhat with Smith's statement that he spent two nights at Santa Catalina, unless we consider that the *Courier* was lying off the island on the night of Jan. 7-8, and left the next evening, events which would put the ship in the proximity of the island for two nights.

[178] Rogers' daybook from this point until it breaks off in late January, was probably the source of many of Smith's specific facts and dates.

again that miserable country and if you do not prepare
yourself well for it it is your own fault. if there is any
thing that you want and that I have let me know and it
shall be at your service. I thanked him for his kindness
and made every exertion to start as soon as possible.
I called on the Commandant to ascertain whether I
could stay longer than the 4 days allowed in my passport he told me a day or two would not make any difference. During my absence one of my Indian guides
who had been imprisoned was released by death and
the other was kept in the guard house at night and at
hard labor during the day having the menial service of
the guard house to perform. I took a convenient opportunity to speak to the Father in his behalf he told me
he would do all in his power for his release. From his
expression I took the idea that goverment had ordered
their imprisonment. the fathers had given me some Iron
and my Smith [179] had made in the shop of the Mission
as many horse shoes as I wanted. He had also given me
some saddles and the leather for rigging them. It was
on the 10th of January 1827 that I returned from St
Diego. The next day I went down to the Courier got
my supplies and returned to the Pueblo Los Angelos
and put up with my friend F Abella commenced
buying horses and in a short time had as many as I

---

[179] Presumably either James Reed or Silas Gobel (*see* Rogers daybook 1
entry for Dec. 1, which names both, or the entry for Jan. 6 which mentions
"our Blacksmith James Reed . . .").

wanted.[180] When I left the Courier I took leave of my friend Capt Cunningham. Should chance ever throw this in his way he will perhaps be gratified to find that I have not forgotten his name or his friendship. That I recollect with the most grateful feelings his kind offices in times that made them doubly valuable and in a country to which he had traveled by the unmarked and perilous paths of the Ocean while my way had been through an unknown Land over mountains and parched inhospitable plains. Meeting in a distant country by routes so different gave an instance of that restless enterprise that has lead and is now leading our countrymen to all parts of the world that has made them travellers on every ocean until it can now be said there is not a breeze of heaven but spreads an american flag. In this place I will give some Ideas in relation to this country of a general nature which may perhaps be interesting. California as I have before observed was settled by Missionaries of the order of St Francis about sixty years since. They established missions in various parts of the country and in civilizing the indians and in imparting to them the benefits of religion they found the opportunity to establish over them the most absolute power. The number of indians under the control of

---

[180] Rogers also came down to Los Angeles to pick up horses and apparently stayed with Francisco Avila, whom he called "Francis St. Abbelo." Dale misread Rogers and came up with a "St. Abbisco" which left him completely bewildered (Dale, 218 n.434). Rogers returned to San Gabriel on Jan. 12; Smith remained at Los Angeles until the 16th (Rogers daybook 1 entries, Jan. 12-16).

each mission varies from 300 to 2000, which are under the care and direction of a priest who is stiled the father and who sometimes has a subordinate or two. The indian has no individual right of Property although he is told that he has an interest in his labors and in the proceeds of the farms and herds of the Mission. He has not the right or at least the power to marry without the consent of the father. for the sexes are not allowed to Labor together during the day and at night they are shut up in separate apartments. And although since the revolution they are by express provision declared free and the fathers were ordered to inform them of the fact yet it does not appear that it has made any material change in their situation. It is not uncharitable perhaps to suppose that the fathers in making known to them their right to freedom have done it in such a way that it appeared to them from their ignorance a change not to be desired. They said to them – I am told – You live in a good country you have plenty to eat to drink and to wear your father takes care of you and will pray for you and show you the way to heaven. On the other hand if you go away from the Missions where will you find so good a country who will give you cloths or where will you find a father to feed you to take care of you and to pray for you. Such arguments as these coming from a source long respected and venerated and acting on the minds of ignorant and superstitious beings has had the effect to keep the indians in their real slavery without the desire of freedom. whatever the causes may be the fact is certain that verry few have availed themselves of the privilege of the revolution. The Missions setting aside their religious professions are in fact Large farming and grazing establishment conducted at the will of the father who is in a certain degree responsible to the President of his order residing in the Province. The immediate supervision of the different kinds of business is confided to Overseers who are generally half Breeds raised in a manner somewhat better than the common mass under the eye of the father from whom they sometimes receive a limited education and to whom in some instances they might with strict propriety apply the name of *father* – The indians are employed in the different kinds of work attendant uppon farming and herding of stock the manufacturing of Blankets of coarse wool which form their principle clothing the making of soap of Brick and in distilling. Their labor does not appear to be unreasonably hard. They are required to attend church regularly every morning after which they immediately move off under the direction of their respective overseers to the business of the day.[181]

Left St Gabriel and moved on toward St Bernardino the most distant farm house belonging to the Mission being about 60 miles from St Gabriel and a few miles south of the route by which I had come in. In three days

---

[181] Nearly two pages in the manuscript are blank, awaiting some later addition which never came.

I arrived at St. Bernardino where I remained several days drying Beef and breaking my young horses as well as looking for some that had strayed away.[182] On leaving father Sanches he directed me to kill Beef and as much as I could dry and to take meal Peas corn wheat or any thing I wanted and such quantities as I chose, in this case as in many others evincing the most benevolent regard for my welfare. Occupied in these preparations for continuing my journey I remained until the 1st day of february 1827 when I left Bernardino accompanied

---

[182] According to Rogers, Smith's party leaves on Jan. 18 and proceeds to La Puente, the rancheria where they had stayed on Nov. 27. On Jan. 19, the group moves on to the next mission farm, Santa Ana del Chino. There they remained until the 21st when the party moves on to the next farm, Jumuba, which was about four miles west of the mission ranch at San Bernardino (The Beatties' book, *Heritage of the Valley,* contains many references to these mission farms.) This route keeps slightly to the south of that by which Smith traveled west through the valley to San Gabriel. The party remains at Jumuba preparing for their trip until at least Jan. 27, when Rogers daybook 1 ends; Smith and Laplant went to San Bernardino on Jan. 22 and 27 for supplies (Rogers daybook 1 entries, Jan. 18-27).

Horses weren't the only strays during these last days in California. John Wilson had been discharged by Smith on Jan. 17, but could not get permission to stay in the country, so "we obliged to let him come back to us. he remains with the company but not under pay as yet. I expect he will not go on with us . . ." (Rogers daybook 1 entry for Jan. 25.) Wilson was let go again in the San Joaquin Valley, a fact Smith does mention later. And Daniel Ferguson (a troublemaker who had been involved in the fight on Jan. 6), perhaps remembering previous hardships and not wanting to forego the comforts of San Gabriel for another stretch on the trail, "on the 18th. Inst. Hide himself and we could not find him. The corporal who commands at the mission promised to find him, and send him to us. But I expect we shall not see him again." (Rogers daybook 1 entry for Jan. 24.) The supposition is correct, although Smith did see Ferguson, and Wilson, again at Monterey on his second trip in the fall of 1827 (Sullivan, *Travels,* 39).

by 2 or three Indians and moved on to the place where I had passed through the Mt and first came in sight of Cattle as I came in to the Beautiful valley of St Gabriel and there I encamped.[183] the indians that came with me thus far killed a Beef. During the night it snowed and in the morning I again moved on nearly north crossing my old track and on the 3d day from Bernardino I had got on the E side of the Mt where there was no snow.* [184] (* It was in this place I first saw a tree I have named the dirk Pear tree.[185] It grows from 15 to 30 feet high 12 inches in diameter wood porous bark rough like the walnut. The leaf like the blade of a dirk is about 8 or ten inches long the point resembling that of a porcupine quill.) I was then obliged to turn my course N W for want of water having the low range of Mts on my left and the barren desert on my right. I encamped without water or grass my horses scattered over the country. I was then forced to look for water and grass and was three days employed in collecting my horses. In this country I had observed some track of the Grizly Bear and the Black tailed deer but they were not numerous.

---

[183] Smith now moves his party northeast toward the San Bernardino Mountains. As other writers have pointed out (for example, Morgan, *Smith,* 206-07), Smith felt that he had complied with Governor Echeandia's orders to leave California by the same route he had entered by departing through the San Bernardino Valley.

[184] See note 122 for details of Smith's route through the mountains.

[185] Smith must have encountered Joshua trees *(Yucca arborescens)* frequently during his transit of Antelope Valley. The few sentences here probably represent the first description of this distinctive plant by an American. In silhouette the large Joshuas do somewhat resemble pear trees, so Smith's name is well taken.

My horses being once more collected I resumed my
N W course for Two short days travel the low Mt still
on my left and Barren plains on my right when I fell
in with some indians who I suppose were runaways
from some mission as they had some horses.[186] I ascertained by enquiry of them that there were some streams
and lakes ahead. I engaged a guide to conduct me to
them and after two days travel still continuing my N W
direction I arrived at a Lake called by the Spaniards
Too Larree or flag Lake.[187] I arrived at the Lake quite

---

[186] After crossing the San Bernardino Mountains, Smith follows the Mojave
River for a short distance, possibly as far as present Victorville, and then
turns northwest keeping the San Gabriel Mountains to his left and the Mojave
Desert to his right. The Burr and Wilkes maps reproduced in Morgan and
Wheat show three small lakes to the right of Smith's route ("fragments of the
playa, Rogers Lake") and two streams running southwest (one of which is
most likely that mentioned in Williamson: ". . . after a long march,
camped on a bold stream which was a river in the foot-hills, but sank immediately upon reaching the Basin. It is marked on Preuss' map from the surveys of Colonel Frémont; but as we knew no name for it, we called it Johnson's River, after the soldier who found it for us." Williamson, 30.) Based
partially on this evidence, Morgan and Wheat reconstructed Smith's route:
"It is evident that from the vicinity of Victorville Jedediah traveled nearly
northwest to the locality of present Mojave, passing through Mirage Valley
and leaving the Shadow Mountains to his right. . . thence into Antelope
Valley. . ." (Morgan and Wheat, *Smith's* Maps, 67.) This projection probably puts Smith too far out into the desert area for it assumes he used
Tehachapi and not Tejon Pass; he could have been aware of the (dried)
lakes even if he had remained closer to the foothills of the mountains.

[187] Smith has now arrived at Kern Lake (so named by John C. Frémont for
Edward M. Kern, the topographer and artist of his third expedition) which
was known to the Spaniards as Tulare because of the rushes (tules) which
crowded its marshy shores. Situated in the southern end of the San Joaquin
Valley, Kern Lake and its neighbor to the west, Buena Vista Lake (both
watered primarily by the Kern River coming out of the Sierra Nevada), were
often united within historic times by fluctuations in the water level. The cir-

late and found the bank so muddy that it was impossible for my horses to get any water yet I was obliged to encamp. From what I could learn of the Indians the Spaniards had named it from report but be that as it may the name was quite appropriate. Too Larre Lake is about 12 miles in circumference and is in a fine Large valley which commences about 12 miles South of it. Coming into the valley from the South East I had passed over a range of hills which in their cours a little East of North appeared to increase in heighth.[188] On

cumference of the combined lakes, however, would have been greater than twelve miles, so undoubtedly Smith is viewing only Kern and is unaware of the existence of Buena Vista. For a partial discussion of the geographical background of the upper San Joaquin Valley, *see* Waldo R. Wedel, *Archeological Investigations at Buena Vista Lake Kern County, Calif.*, 3-9. Smith at this point in his narrative has neglected to mention crossing a mountain range to reach the lake, an omission he soon rectifies.

188 The Tehachapi Mountains, which Smith could have crossed by either of two possible routes. The most accepted theory (Morgan and Wheat, *Smith's Maps*, 67) is that the party used the "old" Tehachapi route – this is, going up into the mountains by way of Oak Creek Pass (rather than the present highway and railroad route through Tehachapi Pass) and then down Tehachapi Creek into the valley near present Caliente (a route used in reverse by Frémont in 1844, for which *see* Donald Jackson and May Lee Spence, *The Expedition of John Charles Frémont*, I, 666-68). However, the other route, and the one which is here proposed as Smith's, uses the "old" Tejon Pass somewhat to the southwest. This passage through the mountains was on a well-used and traditional Indian trail between the Tulare lakes and other Indian settlements to the south, and utilized Tejon Creek as the means of transit through the northern slopes of the mountains. It was explored in detail, and used, by Lt. Williamson (*see* Williamson, 20-22 and 27-28).

The Tehachapi Pass, even using the Oak Creek approach from the desert would be too far to the east for Smith, and would require him to travel out in the desert even farther than he did. It would also put him into the San Joaquin Valley in a position which would have required him to turn back to the south-the declivity of these hills there was some Oak timber. I observed the trees had many holes made in their trunks in which an acorn was pressed so tight that it was difficult to get it out. By watching I found this to be the work of a bird of the woodpecker kind who takes this method to lay up his stock of provision for the winter. The bird is of a seal color and somewhat larger than the red head woodpecker. I called this bird the Provident woodpecker.[189] The following day in moving along the bank of the Lake I surprised some indians who immediately pushed out into the lake in canoes or rather rafts made of flag. My guide succeeded in getting them to return to the shore. One of them could talk

---

west to reach Kern Lake; in fact, by this route he could have completely missed the lake and gone straight north to meet the Kern River near present Bakersfield.

The Tejon Creek Pass was the more direct route to Kern Lake. Smith probably travels northwest from the Mojave River along the edges of the San Gabriels, a trail similar to that projected as the one used in 1772 by Captain Pedro Fages (Herbert E. Bolton, "In the South San Joaquin ahead of Garcés," 211-19). He could meet his Indians and hire the guide in the general area of present Fairmont (Antelope Buttes) where the Tejon Pass trail turned south into the mountains near Elizabeth Lake and followed San Francisquito canyon down into the San Fernando and Santa Clara valleys. Certainly this would be a logical place to fall in with Indians, particularly renegades from the missions. From this point, Smith would move on a route slightly west of north, cut off the end of Antelope Valley, and head for the Tehachapi Mountains which were entered around present White Oaks. The party would then follow Tejon Creek down into the valley and be in good position to see and travel to Kern Lake.

[189] The bird is the Acorn Woodpecker *(Melanerpes formicivorus)*, sometimes known as the California Woodpecker. Its back is more black, however, than "seal color," but it is known for its distinctive habit of storing acorns in the bark of trees (Peterson, 142).

some Spanish and I engaged him for a guide. I watered my horses and got some fish from the indians (who I observed had some horses stolen no doubt from the Spaniards) and moved on about 3 miles along the Lake and then up an inlet about 10 miles crossed over and encamped.[190] On this inlet was some timber Cotton wood and willow. where I crossed it was 8 or 10 yard wide rapid current 2 feet deep and comes from the East. Several Indians some of them having horses visited the encampment. The principal characters brought withe them each a small sack of down and sprinkled me from head to foot. To this I submitted knowing it was a custom among them and wishing to avoid giving offence.[191] The[y] told me of a river to

---

[190] During this day, Smith and his men travel along the eastern perimeter of Kern Lake, encountering some Hometwoli Indians of the Yokuts tribe who inhabited the southern end of the valley around the lake (Kroeber, 478). The rafts were rather curious vessels: "Reconstructed models reveal only a cigar-shaped aggregation of bundles of rush, but the best specimens of the old days may have approximated real boats in having raised edges. . . their light-ness raised the whole mass so high that even the bottom of the hollow was above the water line, the gunwales serving only the convenience of preventing wave wash from entering and load or killed game from slipping overboard. Some of these lake boats carried three or four men in comfort, and could bear a small fire on an earth hearth" (*Ibid.*, 531).

Then the Americans turn north along the south fork of the Kern River, crossing it and encamping near present Bakersfield.

[191] One encounters references to this custom (but usually with seed, as Smith will experience later, rather than down) in several early accounts of the region. Garcés, for one, relates that ". . . the wife of the chief arose, took a basket *(corita)* of seed *(chico)* and scattered it over the Santo Cristo I wore on my breast; the same did other women, and they even threw some of this seed *(semilla)* on the fire. . ." (Coues, I, 276.)

the north that had an animal which I supposed from their description to be the Beaver although they had no name for the animal by which it was known to me. These indians call themselves Wa-ya-la-ma.[192] The indian that spoke spanish and the same I engaged at the flag Lake told me he would go on with me and my other guide returned. On the following day I moved Northwardly 15 miles across low hills which were spurs of the mountain on the East.[193] This mountain had been gradually increasing in elevation and had now attained a considerable heighth. The next day I moved nearly North West 30 miles over a level country the ground being so completely undermined by the paths of an animal like the Lizard that the horses were continually sinking in the Earth frequently up to the nees. I encamped on the bank of a Lake.[194] Since leaving the wa

---

[192] Smith means the Yauelmani Indians, another group of the southern Yokuts who inhabited the southeastern section of the valley, east and north of the Hometwoli whom he met on Kern Lake. A major Yauelmani settlement was Woilo ("planting place" – "sowing place") on the site of Bakersfield (Kroeber, 482). It could well be that this is the spot at which Smith encamped.

[193] The party now travels north along the foothills to a point near or east of present Famoso, possibly about where Poso Creek enters the valley.

[194] Traveling northwest, and possibly keeping generally along the route of Poso Creek, the Americans come to what would be known as Tulare Lake, but which Smith later calls "Chin-ta-che." The name given by Smith (appearing as "Chintache" on the Wilkes and Gibbs maps, and as "Chentache" on Burr's) derives from the Spaniards, who called the lake *Laguna de Tache* after the Tachi (or to the Spaniards, "Sumtache" or "Tuntache") Indians who were to the northwest of the three Yokuts tribes on Tulare Lake (*see* Kroeber, 483-84). At one time occupying a large portion of the central San Joaquin Valley, and watered by streams running in from the Sierra Nevada,

ya la ma the country has been dry and destitute of water and grass. I found water in but one place in the bed of a stream which was nearly dry.[195] East of my route at the foot of the Mt there was some timber and plenty of grass and water. The Lake on which I encamped was apparently large extending to the N W so far that the shore was not visible. But as I supposed it not more than

the lake was surrounded by tule growing on its gradually receding shoreline which was an almost impassable network of brackish sloughs. To avoid this swamp on his second transit of the valley in the fall of 1827, Smith stayed farther east along the foothills according to the route shown in the Gibbs map (there incorrectly labeled "1828") and also on the Burr map. By the time Lt. George Derby passed through the valley in 1850, the lake had shrunk into two – the northern Tache Lake and the southern Ton Tache. For Derby's expedition *see:* Francis P. Farquhar (ed.), "The Topographical Reports of Lieutenant George H. Derby," 252-53.

By not passing this way again, Smith would also avoid crossing the terrain made hazardous by the burrows of the common gray ground squirrel of California *(Spermophilus beechyi)*. Nearly every early traveler here has some account of difficulties caused by the little animals. Garcés relates ". . . we fell down, the mule and myself, and several times I was in danger of the same, because of the insecurity of the ground. In the fall I lost the compass needle, and did not think of returning to search for it, because it made me afraid to see a land so dry and dangerous to travel." (Coues, I, 301.) Frémont complained about the "rotten ground in which the horses were frequently up to their knees" (Jackson and Spence, I, 664), and Derby was equally disenchanted: ". . . the most wretched country that I ever beheld. The soil was not only of the most wretched description, dry, powdery and decomposed, but was everywhere burrowed by gophers, and a small animal resembling a common house rat . . . Their holes and burrows, into which a horse sinks up to his knees at almost every step, render the travelling difficult and dangerous." (Farquhar, "Derby," 255.) It even fell the lot of one group of Indians, the Po-hal'-lin-Tin'-leh (squirrel holes") to receive their name from living in the place (Coues, I, 270).

[195] Again, Poso Creek, which takes its name from the Spanish *pozo* (well), widely used for watering holes.

8o miles to the Ocean I did not think it of verry great
extent. It appeared shallow from the number of Boggy
Islands seen in many parts of it. Near where I encamped was an Indian village of two or three hundred
inhabitants.[196] Their Lodges were built of willows and
Mats. the willows were placed in the ground in rows at
the distance of ten feet apart and bent over and joined
together at the top and then covered with the mats
forming a Lodge in exterior appearance like a line of
barracks and about 100 yards in length with a door at
proper intervals for each family.[197] My provision being
nearly exhausted I visited the village for the purpose
of trading for some provision. My interpreter having
gone before to inform them of my approach when I
arrived some mats were spread in front of the Lodges
and I was invited to sit down. Grass seed was then

---

[196] The village is probably Sukuwutnu, a settlement of the Wowol Yokuts,
located approximately a few miles west of present Delano. The Indians "lived
on an island off the east shore of the lake, from which they had to cross on
their tule rafts to the timbered or brushy stream outlets on the mainland to
obtain firewood. This island is said to have been due west of present Delano,
which identifies it with Atwells Island, where old maps show an Indian
rancheria on the lake shore. This settlement was called Sukuwutnu. . ."
(Kroeber, 483.)

[197] The communal *kawi* was a distinctive type of dwelling employed by
several of the Yokuts tribes including the Wowol. "The roof pitch was steep.
Probably each family constructed its own portion, with door to front and back,
closed at night with tule mats. Each household had its own space and fire-
place, but there were no partitions, and one could look through from end to
end. These houses sometimes ran to a size where they accommodated a little
more than 10 families. A shade porch extended along the front. The tule
stalks were sewn together with an eyed bone needle and string of tule fibre."
(*Ibid.*, 521.)

brought and poured on my head until I was nearly covered. This seed which was gathered during the summer formed at this time the principal subsistenc of these indians. I gave them some presents and after som conversation with the chiefs made arrangement to have my grass seed formed into meal. At night I was invited to attend a dance and went to the Lodge at 8 O Clock and found a seat prepared for me. I was immediately treated with some roasted fish and a mush made of the grass seed. After supper the dancers came in 10 or 12 in number and seated themselves in a cluster. they were painted and some of them had head dresses made of feathers and a skin around the waist. Having remained at this encampment two days I moved north along the beach of the Lake and again encamped,[198] on a low spot of ground on the beach. durring the night a high north west wind raised the water of the Lake and drove it into my encampment so that I was obliged to remove to higher ground. East of this encampment a level country with but little vegetation extends to the foot of the mountain a distance of about 20 miles. On the following day I left the Beach of the Lake as my guide said there was a stream putting in which I could not cross near its mouth I therefore traveled North Eastwardly and at 18 miles encamped on a small River 20 yds wide deep and Muddy with low Oak timber

---

[198] One can only assume that this camp was somewhat southeast of present Pixley perhaps around Deer Creek or just to the north. The group probably retreated to a sand bank left by the receding lake to escape the storm.

along its banks.[199] During the day I saw several antelops and some Elk sign and passed a country like the last described * (* One of my men (John Willson) again manifesting that seditious disposition of which I had before had reason to complain and which could not be suffered consistently with the subordination necessary to the safety of my party I was forced to discharge him. I found two Indians who spoke spanish and engaged them to conduct him to the upper settlement of California which they said they could reach in 3 days.[200]) The next day I crossed the stream carrying my goods over on a Log and swimming my horses and traveled North Eastwardly 12 miles crossing several small streams having oak timber and a plenty of grass on their banks. The soil was verry fine and although somewhat wet yet it produced most excellent grass. The prairae and woodland was mingled in pleasing variety and my encampment was on a small stream in a fine little grove of timber.[201] My guide informed me that in the neighbor-

---

[199] The Indians warned Smith of the difficulties he might expect if he attempted to cross the marshes in the area where the several branches of the Kaweah River entered Tulare Lake. Traveling the direction and distance indicated here would place the camp on the banks of the Tule River, a few miles west of present Porterville.

[200] Smith discharged "Willson" at the Wowol settlements, for upon meeting Wilson in Monterey the next fall, Smith mentioned that he was "discharged at the Chintache Lake" (Sullivan, *Travels,* 39). Wilson was first imprisoned by the Spaniards, but after his release settled down and married (*Ibid.,* 171 n.79; Dale, 223 n.443). *See also* note 182.

[201] Having crossed the Tule, Smith continues on to reach the Kaweah River, probably in the vicinity of present Exeter.

The river received its name because the "Kawia" or "Gawia" members of

hood was a plenty of Elk. I therefore sent some men hunting they killed 2 antelope and found Elk but killed none.

In company with my guide I visited some Indians that were up near the foot of the Mt and at the distance of about 15 miles. Their Lodges were built like those before described at the Chin-ta-che Lake.[202] The country appeared populous but the soil gravelly and not as rich as at the encampment. near the Mt there is a good deal of Oak timber the trees having large trunks but Low and spreading tops so that it is not of the most valuable kind for building or fencing. My guide saying he was unacquainted with the country further north I engaged another who told me that in one day I could travel to where I could find Beaver – Having remained two days at the last mentioned encampment I moved on N Westwardly 25 miles crossing in the course of the day 2 small streams and encamping near a large indian village on the bank of a river 80 yds wide where I found some Beaver sign.[203] These Indians called them-

---

the Yokuts lived on the edge of the plains on its north banks. It was discovered in 1806 by Ensign Gabriel Moraga who called it the San Gabriel; for Derby it became the "Frances."

[202] There are two possibilities for the Indians. The Yokod (or Yokol) had their winter camp on the south bank of the Kaweah, north of present Exeter, and the Wükchmni wintered on the Kaweah around present Lemoncove, closer to the mountains (Kroeber, 480). It is most likely that Smith refers to the Wükchmni, as the distances mentioned would better fit the location of their camp.

[203] One of the two "Small streams" is probably Cottonwood (Cross) Creek, but the identify of the other is even less certain. Smith would arrive at the

selves Wim-mil-che and this name I applied to the river which comes from E N E.[204] In the vicinity was considerable timber (Oak) and a plenty of grass. The game of the country was principally Elk and Antelope. On the 28th of February I commenced trapping on the Wimmilche and during 10 days I moved up the river 25 or 30 miles. I was then near the foot of the Mt and finding no further inducement for trapping and the indians telling me of a river they called the Peticutry in which there was beaver I traveled north along near the foot of the Mt about 15 miles and encamped on the bank of the Peticutry* (* at the place where I first

---

Kings River at a spot somewhere east of Kingsburg; this would be approximately the eastern limit of Wimilchi Indian territory.

[204] The Wimilchi lived on the north bank of the river at this point, and occupied several of the various sloughs which connected the Kings to Tulare Lake (Kroeber, 483). *See also* C. Hart Merriam's comments on their territory in his article, "Jedediah Smith's Route Across the Sierra, in 1827," 25-29.

In his letter of July 12, 1827, to Clark, Smith called the tribe "Wim-mul-che" – or so it was printed in the St. Louis paper (*Missouri Republican,* Oct. 11, 1827). The name enjoyed several variants over the years; for example it becomes "Winmiche" on the Burr map. The river, however, is now called after its traditional Spanish name, *Rio de Los Santos Reyes.* Smith's description of his camp compares remarkably with Frémont's of Apr. 8, 1844, which was in the same general area: "On the opposite side we found some forty or fifty Indians who had come to meet us from the village below. We made them some small presents, and invited them to accompany us to our encampment, which after about three miles through fine oak groves, we made on the river." (Jackson and Spence, 664.)

There is no indication there that Smith attempted to cross the Sierra at this point as his letter to Clark suggests. It is clear that in his letter, Smith is referring to events which later took place on the American River – the deep snow, the loss of horses, and the return to the valley – and he just happened to get the name of his river wrong, a mistake which has misled some later writers (viz. Francis P. Farquhar, *History of the Sierra Nevada,* 26).

struck the Peticutry were a great number of small artificial mounds.) running at this place west and not quite as large as the Wim mil che.[205] In this vicinity the plains are generally clothed with grass and were at that time covered withe Blossoms. Along the river there is some timber. At the foot of the Mt the timber is Oak and far up the Mt Pine.

The Peticutry runs west 10 miles and then turns N N W. I continued trapping down this river about 35 miles after it turned N W. It there received a stream from the East 60 yards wide called the Noto.[206] The

---

[205] As Smith indicates, he follows the Kings River up to the mountains and then turns northwest along the foothills until he comes to the San Joaquin (his "Peticutry") near where it exits the Sierra north of Fresno. Just what the "mounds" are has not been determined. The route Smith describes will have to change some projections made by Morgan and Wheat. Not knowing that Smith turned to go upstream on the Kings, they had him striking directly for the bend of the San Joaquin from this point, basing their theory on the Burr and Gibbs maps (Morgan and Wheat, *Smith's Maps*, 68).

Even though Smith gives a definite date, Feb. 28, for the start of his trapping along the Kings, it is impossible to use this in establishing any satisfactory daily chronology for the preceding month; there is about a six-day error between established dates.

Smith's name for the San Joaquin, "Peticutry," appears to derive from Indians who lived in the vicinity of preent Herndon, the Pitkachi (plural Kitakati, or Pidekati) (Kroeber, 484).

[206] The "Noto" is today's Merced River (so named by Ensign Moraga in 1806, *Rio de Nuestra Señora de la Merced*), which Smith reaches after following the San Joaquin west and then north. The party seems to have remained on the south – and later west – bank of the river according to the Burr and Gibbs maps (Morgan and Wheat, *Smith's Maps*, 68).

Smith names the river after some Southern Miwok Indians, the Nototemnes; Fr. Narciso Durán of Mission San José mentions encountering a tribe in this general area in 1817 to which he gave that name (Kroeber, 445).

Peticutry had received some small streams from the
East above the bend the banks were high and the current rapid but below the river had ben divided into
many small Slous and channels the banks low and the
current sluggish. In many places Flags rushes and mud
a mile in width made it impassible for horses. On the
Noto was a good deal of timber Oak and some Ash.
After passing the Noto ten miles Otter river comes in
from the E.[207] It is about 60 yds wide and much resembles the Noto. From the Wim-mil-che a range of hills
has extended nearly paralel with my course.[208] Leaving
the valley from the foot of the Mt measureing west
about 40 miles in width. Six miles beyond Otter river
comes in another of the same size from the East which
I called the Appelaminy.[209] Since passing the Wim-
milch there had been an abundance of Elk and some
Antelope and on the West side of the Peticutry plenty
of wild horses. Birds of the larger kinds were numerous

[207] The Tuolumne River, which takes its name from a band of Central
Miwok Indians. The stream appears on the Frémont-Preuss map of 1848 as
the *Rio de los Towalumnes.*

[208] Smith probably refers to the Diablo Range which rises along the course
of the San Joaquin to the west. He is correct in estimating that the valley in
this area is about forty miles wide.

[209] The Stanislaus River. "Appelaminy" must be of Indian derivation, considering how Smith names most other rivers in the valley. The probable source
is "Ochehamni," a Plains Miwok tribe in the area (Kroeber, 444); these are
the Ochejamnes of Durán (*Ibid.,* 445).

The river was discovered in 1806 by Moraga who called it *Rio de Nuestra
Senora de Guadalupe.* In 1827 or 1828, a neophyte named Estanislao ran away
from San José and eventually became leader of some Indians who were
defeated at the stream by Mariano Vallejo in 1829; hence the Stanislaus.

and particularly birds of passage as this was their season. I saw wild Geese White and Grey Brant Blue and White Heron Cormorant many kinds of Ducks and common Buzzard. Hawks of all Colors. Magpyes. A kind of Pigeon resembling the tame Blue Pigeon 2 or Three kinds of Eagles and a verry larg Bird which I supposed to be the Vulture or the Condor.[210] Small birds were quite scarce and I saw verry few snakes. The Peticutry would be navigable for large boats as far up as the bend near the Mt.[211] The country Generally is a most excellent grazing country. On the Peticutry noto Otter and Appelamminy Rivers the soil is such as to admit of many fine farms. There might be in places a want of timber but the neighboring Mountain would afford an ample supply which could be easily floated down the streams almost to any desired point Since I struck the Peticutry I had seen but few indians. The greater part of those that once resided here having (as I have sinc been told) gone in to the Missions of St Joseph and Santa Clara.[212]

----

[210] Of the birds mentioned, only one or two are not self-evident. The pigeon is the Band-Tailed Pigeon *(Columba fasciata)*, a bird closely resembling its more domestic cousin, the Rock Dove (Peterson, 113). There is no reason why Smith could not have encountered the famed California condor *(Gynmogyps californianus)* here for it is occasionally found in the western foothills of the Sierra *(Ibid.,* 47-48).

[211] Smith refers to a point approximately at present Firebaugh; his prophesy hinges on what he meant by "large boats."

[212] The Mission San José de Guadalupe was about fifteen miles from the pueblo (and later city) of the same name. The church, by then in disrepair, was destroyed by an earthquake in 1868. Mission Santa Clara de Asís later

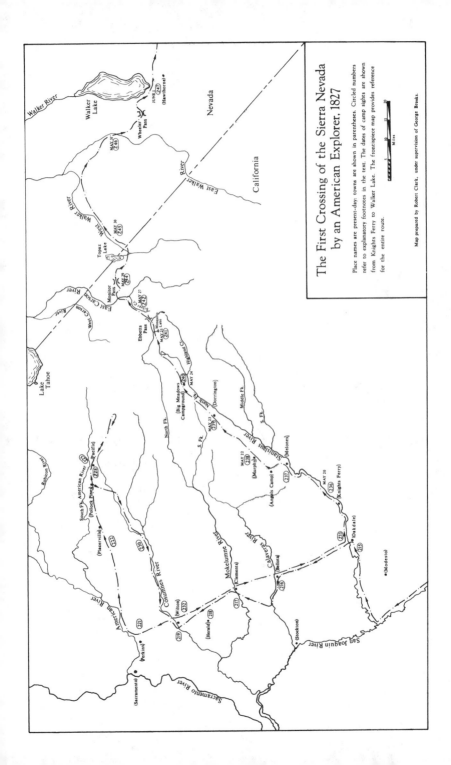

The First Crossing of the Sierra Nevada by an American Explorer, 1827

Place names are present-day; towns are shown in parentheses. Circled numbers refer to explanatory footnotes in the text. The dates of camp sights are shown from Knights Ferry to Walker Lake. The frontispiece map provides reference for the entire route.

Map prepared by Robert Clark, under supervision of George Brooks.

The Mountain on the East which I called St Joseph in honor of one of the best of men father Joseph Sances of St Gabriel [213] had been gradually increasing in heighth from the place where I crossed its southern extremity near the Too Larree Lake and running north and nearly parallel with the General course of my travel had for some distance attained a most tremendous heighth. The summits could hardly ever be seen as they rose far into the region of perpetual snow and were generally enveloped in clouds. But when the clouds for a while passed away and brought the Peaks to view rising from their dark base covered with snow and gleaming in the sun they possessed an unsurpassed grandeur and Sublimity.

On leaving my partners in the Mountains to go into an unknown country It had been my intention to return at the expiration of my falls hunt or if this was found impracticable by the 1st of July of the following year 1827. Circumstances already related having rendered it impossible for me to join them at the first mentioned time and the second being rapidly approaching It became necessary that I shoul[d] begin making arrangements for marching Eastward toward the Rendevous

---

became the nucleus of the Jesuit college which occupies the site today; the church was destroyed by fire in 1926.

[213] Smith's statement once and for all clears up what had been a long-standing difference of opinion between Francis Farquhar and Dale Morgan (*see* Farquhar, *History of the Sierra Nevada*, 27 n.4). As Morgan contended, Smith named the entire Sierra Nevada chain for Fr. Sánchez of San Gabriel and not for the Mission San José.

in the Mountains which I then looked on as a home. I had several packs of Beaver and the month of April was nearly gone.[214] Mt St Joseph on the East and between me and the rendezvous presented in its appearance an inpassible Barrier. I determined I would leave the Peticutry and ascend the appelamminy to the Mountain and then proceed north along its base and endeavor to find a pass. Accordingly I ascended the appelamminy to the foot of the Mt a distance of about 35 miles and the course generally East.[215] The country like the last described. I then traveled north at the base or among the spurs of the Mt" about 20 miles where I struck a river about 30 yds wide rapid current and running N W. On this river which I called the Mac-al-lum-bry indians appeared quite numerous amounting to several hundred Lodges and residing in several different villages. their Lodges were small and built of dirt.[216]

---

[214] It was probably more like the middle of April, based on a very rough estimate of the party's movements.

[215] The group is now ascending the Stanislaus to a point in the general vicinity of present Oakdale.

[216] Continuing northwest at the foot of the Sierra, Smith and his men reach the Calaveras River, probably around present Bellota. Apparently the transcriber has made another error in copying directions; the river flows southwest and not "NW."

The Indians for whom Smith names the river are the Mokelumne, a division of the Northern Miwok, although the river which today bears their name is the next important stream to the north. The Northern Miwok occupied the land drained by the Calaveras and Mokelumne rivers (Kroeber, 442), Gudde, *California Place Names*, 49, identifies the stream with a river called the Yachicume (after Yatchicomnes Indians, another of those tribes met by Fr.

On the Appelamminy I had engaged a guide to come with thus far who spoke some spanish. I had a consultation with the chiefs and made them some presents and procured another guide who was like the most of those I had had befor a runaway from some Mission. I then moved down the Macallumbry 12 miles and turning from it to the North East in 15 miles I struck a stream 30 yds wide rocky and rapid running west. This stream I called Rock River.[217] In crossing it I had a good deal of difficulty. One of my horses was swept down by its rapid current and the load consisting of 12 traps was lost. I was detained a day in searching for my traps but without sucess, and my guide ran away taking with him two of my horses. In the course of the day 8 or 10 Indians showed themselves on a high hill. They were apparently strangers and knew not what to think of us as I supposed by their actions. They were naked and had their Bows and arrows in their hands. I went to them alone and gave them some presents and they went off. The country since leaving the Appelamminy has been rough my course having been over the spurs of the Mt the timber Oak and rather scrubby plenty of grass and water a fine grazing country. Leaving Rock River I traveled N W down into the plain and passed several

---

Duran in 1817) mentioned by Frederick W. Beechey, the English explorer, in the narrative of his 1826 expedition to the Bering Sea.

Calaveras is after the Spanish, *Arroyo de las Calaveras* (skull creek).

[217] Smith travels down the Calaveras, possibly to avoid the foothills to the north, and then cuts back to meet his "Rock River," today's Mokelumne. He probably crosses the river at a point somewhat west of present Clements.

indian villages. Each village consisting of 30 or 40 small dirt Lodges the indians verry wild ran screaming into the woods.* (* These indians as well as some others may be called Grass eaters. they subsist to a certain extent on clover wild Pea vines and some other herbs which are prepared for eating by wilting them on hot stones.) The first six miles of the days travel was in the spurs of the Mt. I then descended into the plain and traveled 9 miles alternately through groves of Oak Prairaes and Meadows of Blue Clover watered by small streams.[218] The game of this vicinity in the Mts is Blk tailed Deer and in the plains Antelope. In the course of the day when I saw the indians so wild I took a man with me and pursued a couple of females and overtook them my object being to convince them of our friendship. I gave them some awls and beads at the same time endeavoring to convince them that I did not wish to hurt them but our parley was broken off by a party of indians who rushed from their concealment close at hand and with intentions apparently not the most friendly made it necessary for us to rejoin the party without delay. At another time during this day I rode a short distance ahead of the Party and was waiting in a small grove for them to come up. At a small

---

[218] Smith travels through the territory of the shy Northern Miwoks, whose occasional experiences with Spaniards from the coast probably were sufficient cause for their retiring behavior. It is an area whose natural beauty also attracted special attention from Frémont in 1844 (*see* Jackson and Spence, I, 658-59), although he records no Indians. Smith's camp would be somewhere in the vicinity of present Herald.

distance I saw an indian and beckened to him to come
to me. He advanced slowly chatting and making many
signs to divert my attention. I was somewhat suspicious
and kept a good look out and in a moment I found
myself nearly surrounded by a considerabl party I immediately gave my horse the spur and left my sociable
friend to converse with those that could better understand him. On the following day I moved N W 12 miles
across a prairae and encamped on a river 40 yds wide
running S W.[219] Some Oak timber and a considerabl
Beaver sign. My men went out to set straps and soon
I heard the cry of the indians the men from below coming in at full speed and saying that two of them had
been attack by the indians and narrowly escaped. Some
men were above setting their traps. I immediately sent
Arthur Black for them but before they got in they were
closely pressed. I had the horses tied up and each man
his saddle horse ready for mounting and a double guard.
But the indians gave us no opportunity to punish them
as they were all soon on the other side of the river which
was not fordable. The next morning early I took six
men and went for the traps that had been set before the
alarm. I found some of them but a good many had been
taken by the indians who showed themselves on the
opposite side of the river. and one venturing within

[219] Smith arrives at the Cosumnes River (so named later for a Miwok
village) which he calls "Indian" because of subsequent events. His camp,
based on directional and distance projection, was in the region of present
Wilton.

long shot was fired at by a Rifleman and killed.[220]
I moved up the River which I called indian River 3
miles and finding a ford crossed over and leaving the
river traveled north about 12 miles when I struck another River Running W S W 100 yds wide rapid current and stony bottom.[221] A considerable body of Oak

---

[220] It may have been this incident (or possibly one a few days later on the
American River) which caused Fr. Durán at San José to write Comandante
Ignacio Martínez at San Francisco on May 16, 1827: "These men [i.e. Smith's
party] have been in the rancherias of the Muguelemnes and Cossmines several
days and their stay brought about this inconvenience to this mission, which
may be the beginning of such troubles and happenings in other missions.
I believe them to be the same people who were at San Gabriel, and who have
come all along the chain of missions causing trouble." (Quoted in Morgan,
Smith, 208-09; original in Bancroft Library, Archivo del Arzobispado de San
Francisco, part v, 27-33. Translation from Sullivan). Comandante Martínez
wrote Governor Echeandia on May 21: ". . . in the rancheria of the
gentile Muquelemes they [Smith's men] were surrounded for battle, but the
Americans forming into square bodies killed five gentiles; these seeing they
were not our soldiers became appeased." (Also quoted in Morgan, *Smith,* 417,
and from Bancroft Library, Archivo del Arzobispado de San Francisco, part
I, 33.)

[221] After going up the Cosumnes to his fording place, Smith strikes north
to reach and encamp on the American River, probably around present Rose-
mont. When Smith passed this way again on Feb. 20, 1828, he wrote: "I went
with the Trappers within a mile of the place where I struck the river on the
last Ap." (Sullivan, *Travels,* 63.) Because Smith's camp in 1828 was almost
at the confluence of the American and Sacramento rivers, Farquhar interprets
this passage to mean that Smith's 1827 camp was one mile from where the
rivers meet (Farquhar, *History of the Sierra Nevada,* 26). However, Smith's
1828 statement indicates that he traveled with the trappers some (unspecified)
distance along the American before nearing the campsite; it was certainly
more than a mile from the confluence, therefore.

Smith gave the American the name "Wild" not because of the stream's own
characteristics, which would have been appropriate, but because of an incident
on Mar. 1, 1828. A young Indian girl apparently fell dead of fright as the

timber along its banks Indians by hundreds but wilder than antelopes running and screaming in every direction. It appeared to me that the farther I traveled north the indians became more numerous. The River on which I encamped I called wild River. I determined to change my course and make a trial towards passing the mountain. I supposed that the snow had become sufficiently hard by that time to bear my horses. I therefore turned East and at first traveled up wild River and then took the divide between wild and Indian Rivers. for the first two days I found no snow the traveling not worse than might be expected. The timber thus far principally Oak and on the second day some verry large cedar. Indians were numerous and I was frequently passing their little villages of 10 or 12 little circular Lodges made of old trees and bark.[222] During these two

Americans galloped after her and overran her tribe in an effort to give them presents. ". . . in commemoration of the singular wildness of those indians and the novel occurence that made it appear so forcibly I named the River on which it happened Wild River. To this River I had before that time applied a different name." (Sullivan, *Travels,* 66.) Smith's other name has not yet come to light.

The Indians mentioned are members of the Southern Maidu, whose territory included the drainage of the American River (*see* Kroeber, 391-441, for his chapter on the Maidu).

[222] Smith now begins his abortive attempt to cross the Sierra by means of an American River route.

One can only guess at parts of the trail, but it seems, in general, to follow what was later known as the Placerville Road and more recently as Highway 50, using the heights between the South Fork of the American and the North Fork of the Cosumnes. There is no way of knowing where the party turns off from the American; one can only suppose that it might be about present Alder Creek (the U.S. Highway 50 turn-off), and that two days' travel brings the

days the indians collected in great numbers around me at two different times. I endeavored to convince them of my disposition to be friendly by every means in my power but to no purpose. They considered all my friendly signs caused by my own weakness. Of our guns they had never seen the effects and supposed them solid sticks which we could only use in close contest. Whatever may have been their views they pressed so closely and in such numbers on my party that I was obliged to Look for an advantageous piece of ground on which to make a stand against the threatened danger. Having found a favorable position I again tried to convince them of my friendly disposition but to no purpose. Their preparations were still going forward and their parties were occupying favorable points around me. Seeing what must be the inevitable consequence I determined to anticipate them in the commencement and wishing to them as little harm as possible and yet consistant with my own safety I ordered 2 men to fire (of course not the most uncertain marksmen). I prefered long shots that it might give them the idea that we could kill at any distance. At the report of the guns both men firing at once two indians fell. For a moment

---

party somewhere in the vicinity of what is now Placerville. Along the way Smith passes small villages of Maidu dwelling along the western slope of the Sierra in their *hübo,* "a conical hut, 10 to 15 feet across, supported by several poles leaned and tied together over a shallow excavation. Bark, sticks, slabs from dead trees, pine needles, and leaves in any combination kept out the weather more or less successfully. . . The disturbed earth was banked up the sides as far as it would reach, some 2 or 3 feet. Occasionally a more pretentious home had a center post." (Kroeber, 408.)

the indians stood still and silent as if a thunder bolt had
fallen among them then a few words passed from party
to party and in a moment they ran like Deer. The other
afray was similar to the above described except that
more guns were fired and more Indians were killed.[223]
I had been gradually rising as I advanced in the Mt and
on the 3d day left the Oak timber and arrived among
the Pine some of which was verry large the hemlock
and the snow. I found the snow so solid that my horses
did not sink in it more than a foot. In the ascent of
the mountain among the oak timber there was some
Black Tailed deer but in the region of the snow no
living animal was seen unless it might be the Mt Pheas-
ant which made a lonely sound like that of Striking on
a muffled drum at intervals of 2 seconds.[224] My encampment of the third night was where the snow was about
3 feet deep.[225] On the 4th I started early directly on
the Divid E and turning S E. Snow increasing in depth
as we advanced and becoming less compact timber had
disappeared except a little hemlock that grew in the

[223] *See* note 220. This incident may have had some bearing on the Spaniards' concerns, but it is only a remote possibility because of the location.

According to a map in Kroeber (plate 37), Placerville (the site of Indak,
Ibid., 294) and the flat or terrace extending slightly to the east was the upland
limit of Maidu settlement. The encounter, therefore, must have taken place in
this area as Smith avoids it on his descent a few days later.

[224] The common Ruffled Grouse *(Bonasa umbellus),* probably seen here in
its reddish version. As Peterson described it, "The male's drumming suggests
a distant motor starting up. The muffled thumping starts slowly, accelerating
into a whir." (Peterson, 63.)

[225] The camp must have been somewhere along the ridge between present
Pollock Pines and Pacific, possibly near Fresh Pond.

deep ravine. Still in advancing the snow became deeper
and less compact and when I had got about 12 miles
from my encampment the horses began to sink so deep
as to render the prospect of proceeding verry doubtful.
we were not yet at the highest part of the Mt and the
distances across was unknown. This was our situation
when news came up from the rear that some of the
horses had given out being able to proceed no further.[226]
It was at once apparent that If I proceeded farther
I should be obliged to leave my horses or at least the
greater part of them and as we knew not how far the
Mountain extended to the East it was more than probable that in attempting to cross it we might ourselves
be lost. On the other hand should I retrace my steps
I would be obliged to pass among indians highly exas-
perated against us who if not warlike were sufficiently
numerous if acting in concert to surround our little
party and kill us with clubs and should I be so fortunate
as to return to the foot of the Mountain in safety what
could I do. To travel north seemed useless for far as
I could see with my glass the Mt seemed to increase in
heighth offering no probability of a pass. To return
around the Mountain South by the way of St Gabriel
would take so much time that I could not possible

[226] Smith's general route takes him east from the ridge ("directly on the
divid") overlooking the South Fork of the American (the "deep ravine" along
which hemlock grow), and then starts to turn southeast probably in the direction of Iron Mountain Ridge where, at some point, the forward progress
ceases. Certainly the topography would seem to support this suggestion.

arrive at the Depo in season to meet my partners. These reflections were passing rapidly through my mind as I stood on a high Peak a mile in advance of my party having called a halt for the purpose of viewing the prospect before me.[227] Far as the eye could see on every side high rugged Peaks arose covered with Eternal snow turning to the East the frozen waste extending rough and desolate beyond the boundaries of vision warned me to return. Below the deep Rocky ravines resounded with immense Cascades and waterfalls where the melting snow and ice was fast hastening to the fertile Plain. The sight in its extended range embraced no living being except it caught a transient glimpse of my little party awaiting my return in the snows below. It was indeed a freezing desolation and one which I thought should keep a man from wandering. I thought of home and all its neglected enjoyments of the cherfull fireside of my father house of the Plenteous harvest of my native land and visions of flowing fields of green and wide spread Prairaes of joyous bustle and of busy life thronged in my mind to make me feel more strongly the utter desolateness of my situation. And is it possible thought [I] that we are creatures of choice and that we follow fortune through such paths as these. Home with contented industry could give us all that is attainable and fortune could do no more.

---

[227] There are several heights in the area which could serve as a lookout, but exact identification of Smith's "high Peak" is impossible.

Surely of all lives the hunters is the most precarious, we endure all the extremes of heat and cold hunger and thirst our lives and property are always at hazard. when we lay down our guards must be placed our Rifles by our sides and our Pistols under our heads ready to spring up at once from our wakeful sleep. I did not indulge in these reflections longer than I have been employed in writing them and they are here as they existed in that hour of trying fortune and will be remembered as long as I live. But the recollection that my party were entirely depending on my movements broke my reverie and convinced me of the necessity of immediate and powerful exertion to extricate myself and party from surrounding difficulties. I suddenly came to the resolution that I would retrace my steps Back in to the valley and to the Appelamminy. by this time as the season was advancing the snow would become more compact * (*There may be some who are not aware of the fact that the snow on those mountains that are continually covered with it in mid summer becomes more solid and compact than in the depth of winter   It is for this reason principally that the summer is the most favorable time to cross snowy mountains.) but as time would not allow me to go on with my whole party I would take 2 men and light horses leaving my property and the remainder of my party on the Appelamminy and make another attempt to cross the Mt and go to the Depo. Should I be so fortunate as to go through I would take a new supply of Men and

Goods and return again to the Appelamminy and endeavor to learn something of this new and unfortunate country. This conclusion was quickly formed and I immediately descended from the Peak and returned to my party. I told my men of the dismal prospect ahead and of the necessity of turning back. We then immediately commenced our retrograde movement and encamped somewhat west of the place on which we had encamped the night before.[228] On the north at a short distance was a considerable branch of wild river running in a tremendous gulph and beyond was a Peak that seemed to rise far above any other part of the Mt. Among many lofty Peaks it seemed the Giant of the scene. To this summit I had the vanity to attach my name.[229] If an honor it was dearly won as those will admit whose fortune it may be hereafter to follow my steps. On the following day we continued back on the trail until we came to a place where there was some grass and there encamped. Having no provision we killed a horse to eat. remaining at this place two days for the purpose of recruiting my fatigued and starved horses I then moved on towards the plain but instead of keeping the route by which I had come up I turned

---

[228] That is back to the ridge overlooking the South Fork of the American, in the Pacific-Pollock Pines area.

[229] Pyramid Peak, up near Lake Tahoe, could perhaps fill the specifications for Smith's personal mountain if he looked across the "gulph" of the American's South Fork in a northeast direction. The Gallatin map of 1836 shows a "Smith's Peak" north of Smith's 1827 route, and the Wilkes map has a "Mt. Smith" in this general location (*see* Morgan and Wheat, *Smith's Maps*).

south and traveled along indian River and in two days arrived in the valley.[230] In the course of this time as I was riding ahead of the party I rose to the top of a small hill. An indian was carelessly walking at a short distance. he heard the sound of my horses feet. turning his head he saw me. he sprang ran a few steps. his bow and arrows flew from his hands he staggered and fell on his face. I went to him turned him over he was apparently lifeless but presently recovered so far as to open his eyes. I put a piece of Tobacco in his hand and left him without being able to make him stand or even sit up. After I had encamped several Indians and this one among the rest came and sit down on an adjoining hill. I went to them gave them some small and endeavored to make them understand that it was my wish to be friendly. They slept near camp all night but I would not allow them to come in although they appeared quite willing to do so. Shortly after this riding along close by the river in turning a short bend I came suddenly on a lodge of indians and took them by surprise some of them plunged into the river and swam away. two or three women more thoughtful than the rest concluded they might save themselves and some of their property by the following expedient. they sent an old man to detain us by chat while they took such things

---

[230] Afraid to return via the Placerville area because of belligerent Indians, Smith could turn south at Pollock Pines, fall onto Clear Creek in the general direction of Pleasant Valley, and then continue on down the North Fork of the Cosumnes, and later the main stream into the valley.

as they could handily get hold off and sliped under cover of the Lodge to the river and swam over to a little island holding the dishes under the water. Without attempting to disturb them I let the old man know that I saw what was going on and also that we were hungry. He brought us some acorn mush * (* This is a common dish of this country. The acorns are hulled pounded into meal and made into mush. It is Boiled in dishes by the help of hot stones. If they have no dishes they make a hole in the ground and line its sides with clay. In many parts of this country acorns appear to be the principal subsistence. In my tour into the mountains I saw in places where there was not more than 5 or 6 Lodges 3 or 4 hundred Bushels cribed ready for use.[231]) I gave him something in return and went to the Lodge. Those that had not yet ran off were skulking about like children playing hide and seek. After endeavoring to quiet their fears I left them & have no

---

[231] The Indians were probably Maidu, although some could have been Miwok; in any case the two groups followed similar practices with acorns (Kroeber, 410-11). A Miwok acorn granary is illustrated in Kroeber, plate 38, and was "an outdoor affair, a yard or so in diameter, a foot or two above the ground, and thatched over, beyond reach of a standing person, after it was filled . . . The natural branches of a tree sometimes were used in place of posts. There was no true basket construction in the cache; the sides were sticks and brush lines with grass, the whole stuck together and tied where necessary. No door was necessary; the twigs were readily pushed aside almost anywhere, and with a little start acorns rolled out in a stream. Even the squirrels had little difficulty in helping themselves at will. . . The Miwok pound acorns with pestles in holes in granite exposures; on flat slabs laid on or stuck into the ground without basketry hopper; and grind them by crushing and rubbing on similar slabs." (*Ibid.*, 447-48.)

doubt but the departure was more pleasant to them than the arrival. On our arrival in the valley we were much fatigued and hungry having for six days had but little to eat except the colt and one Beaver. At night however we got some trap set. In my Promenade into the Mountain I had gone about 60 miles from the base lost 6 horses and learned one thing which I did not know before that I must be sometime turned back. In the morning we had caught several Beaver and of course had something good to eat much better than the flesh of the poor colt. Continuing to march down Indian River I crossed it in the place where I had before crossed as I traveled north in doing which the horse on which my ammunition was packed stepping in the middle of the River and breaking loose from the leader was washed down below the ford drowned and sunk in the deep water.[232] This was indeed a terrible blow for if our ammunition was lost with it went our means of subsistence and we were at once deprived of what enabled us to travel among hostile bands feared and respected. But my thoughts I kept to myself knowing that a few words from me would discourage my men. I immediately set 2 men on the bank of the river to watch knowing this fact without knowing the reason that a horse unless kept down by a heavy load will rise to the surface in from 10 to 30 minutes. By the time the party had crossed over the men on the bank told me

---

[232] *See* note 219. Smith's party crossed the Cosumnes near present Wilton on their northward journey.

they thought they could see one of the horses feet the
load keeping the animal from floating off. One of the
men who was a good swimmer went in and fastening a
cord the whole was pulled out together. Besides Lead
there was 25 or 30 lbs of powder in the pack but as it
was in a good leather sack but a part of it was damaged.
Although this happened within three miles of the place
where the indians had manifested their hostility by
attacking my trappers and stealing my traps yet there
was not an indian to be seen – On the following day
I traveled South and encamped a short distance North
of Rock River in the course of the day I killed an Elk.
At Rock River I was detained a day having to make a
raft and meeting with some difficulty in crossing. The
next south to the McKalumbry and the following day
to the Appelamminy passing a good many Elk and
killing one fine fat doe. I then moved up the Appelaminy a few miles to a place where I found a suitable
place and encamped with the intention of remaining
several days in order to make the necessary preparations for my journey across the Mt to the Depo.[233] The
time was employed in pressing and cacheing my furs

[233] During his southbound trip, Smith generally retraces his steps and
crosses the "Rock" (the Mokelumne, but without mentioning that Indians stole
his horses) and the "McKalumbry" (Calaveras) rivers before moving on to
what would become a permanent encampment for most of his men on the
"Appelaminy" (Stanislaus).
The camp on the Stanislaus was probably in the vicinity of Oakdale, as
Smith later mentions traveling east twelve miles from there to reach to "foot
of the mountain," presumably meaning by that a place somewhere around
present Knights Ferry.

killing Game and drying meat shoeing some horses and making some hay to feed them in the Mt* (*while at this place the Mackalumbry chief brought one of the horses stolen from me on Rock River. I gave him some presents and he engaged to bring the other.[234])

I gave Mr Rodgers instructions to remain in the vicinity leaving a note at the cache with directions that would enable me to find him whenever I should return. If the 20th of September should arrive without my return he might then consider me dead. In that case he was to proceed to Bodega and get supplies and if possible make his way to the Depo.[235] If this was found

---

[234] Of the chief, and this incident, Smith wrote the next year: "The old Macalumbry Chief (Te-mi), of whom I have before spoken [i.e. this reference here], frequently visited them [Rogers and his men], bringing them grass seid meal, currents and raspberries &c, and they in return loaded him with meat, which appeared to the indians of this country a most acceptable present.

"Among other incidents It may not be amiss to mention that Te-Mi brought the stolen horse, as he had promised, a few days after I started for the Depo. He had also brought 7 or 8 of the traps lost in Rock River that had been broken in pieces by the indians, but the men had repaired them" (Sullivan, *Travels,* 35-36).

[235] Smith actually returned to Rogers and his men on August 15, 1827 (Sullivan, *Travels,* 25), so there was no need for that group to go on to the Russian post on Bodega Bay.

Omissions are sometimes as perplexing as what is included in this journal, and here Smith neglects to mention two important aspects in his story. It was at this point in his journey, on May 19, that Smith wrote his often reproduced letter to Fr. Durán at San José:

"Reverend Father: —— I understand, through the medium of one of your Christian Indians, that you are anxious to know who we are, as some of the Indians have been at the Mission and informed you that there were certain white people in the country. We are Americans, on our journey to the River Columbia; we were in at the Mission San Gabriel in January last; I went to

impracticable he was then to dispose of his property wait an opportunity to ship to the sandwich Islands and from thence to the United States. On the 20th of May 1827 my preparations being finished I took leave of my small but faithful party and started on an enterprise involved in great uncertainty. I took but two men with me Robert Evans and Silas Goble. I had six horses and two mules. I had about 60 lbs of meat and a part of my horses were packed with hay to feed them during the passage of the Mountains.* (*three men accompanied me with some extra horses.) Traveling east 12 miles I stoped at the foot of the Mt for dinner and then con-

-----

San Diego and saw the General, and got a passport from him to pass on to that place. I have made several efforts to cross the mountains, but the snow being so deep, I could not succeed in getting over. I returned to this place (it being the only point to kill meat) to wait a few weeks until the snow melts so that I can go on; the Indians here also being friendly, I consider it the most safe point for me to remain, until such time as I can cross the mountains with my horses, having lost a great many in attempting to cross ten or fifteen days since. I am a long ways from home, and am anxious to get there as soon as the nature of the case will admit. Our situation is quite unpleasant, being destitute of clothing and most necessities of life, wild meat being our principal subsistence. I am, Reverend Father, your strange, but real friend and Christian brother, *J. S. Smith*" (The text, which recognizably adjusts the truth, is taken from Morgan, *Smith,* 333, who in turn took it from Dale, 230-31).

Sometime immediately prior to this, Smith also elected to take Silas Gobel and Robert Evans with him as his two companions in the attempt to return to the depot. Just why he selected these two is never explained, and presumably will never be known.

In any event, Smith is now encamped on the Stanislaus, ready to make his crossing of the Sierra by a route which will take him through Ebbetts Pass as correctly hypothesized by Farquhar with stunning accuracy in "Jedediah Smith and the First Crossing of the Sierra Nevada," 35-52 (and later expanded upon in his *History of the Sierra Nevada,* 23-29).

tinued on N N E 13 miles through very rough traveling and encamped on the North side of the Appelminy.[236] Some friendly indians were seen in the course of the day.

21st   N E 30 miles following the river the traveling rough rugged and mountainous.[237]

22nd   12 miles N E   In the morning the three men that had come with me thus far returned and I struck out from the River. Saw no indians although we heard the yell of some on the opposite side of the river when we left camp.[238]

23rd   20 miles N N E passed several indian lodges but as is the custom here the indians ran off yelling and shouting. I encamped on the divide between Rock River and the Appelamminy.[239]

---

[236] Much of the projection of this day's travel depends on what Smith means by the "foot of the mountain" as roughly the mid-point in the journey. It would seem, however, in considering the whole trip over the Sierra that he reaches a campsite someplace in the present Tulloch Lake area.

[237] The course of the river upstream from Tulloch Lake is tortuous, and certainly the terrain is "rough rugged and mountainous." Smith probably gets as far as the general vicinity of Angels Creek or perhaps as far as present Melones before halting.

[238] The Angels Creek – Melones area would be a logical point to turn away from the Stanislaus, and Smith passes near the present towns of either Angels Creek or Vallecito depending on his point of departure. By either way, he eventually reaches a spot near the present town of Murphy for his camp on May 22.

[239] Continuing approximately along what is now Route 4 (the Ebbetts Pass Road), Smith, Gobel, and Evans probably get to Summit Level Ridge in the general area of present Dorington for their day's travel.

24th   15 miles N E   following the divide at 8 miles
from Camp I came to the snow which soon increased
to 4 feet in debth but so solid that the horses did not
sink in it more than 6 or 8 inches. at night I found a
place where the ground was bare and a little grass
growing on a southern slope of a Mt there I encamped.[240]

25th   18 miles N E   Keeping the divide and over the
snow which soon increased to the debth of 8 feet at
3 O Clock it turned cold and commenced snowing.
I was obliged to encamp found a few pines for shelter
tied up my horses to keep them from running away and
gave them some of the hay I had packed from the
valley. During the night the storm increased in violence
and the weather became extremely cold.[241]

26th   The Storm still continued with unabated violence. I was obliged to remain in camp. It was one of
the most disagreeable days I ever passed. We were
uncertain how far the Mountain extended to the East.
The wind was continually changing and the snow drifting and flying in every direction. It was with great
difficulty that we could get wood and we were but just
able to keep our fire. Our poor animals felt a full share

---

[240] The route still continues along Summit Level Ridge and Route 4, and
one can only estimae that perhaps Smith finds his "little grass growing on a
southern slope" near what is now Big Meadow.

[241] If these projections hold, Smith and his companions bog down and become snowbound somewhere near Pacific Grade Summit, which is almost at
the ultimate source of the North Fork of the Stanislaus and less than a mile
from the headwaters of the Mokelumne.

of the vengeanc of the storm and 2 horses and one mule froze to death before our eyes. Still the storm continued with unabated violence and it required an utmost exertion to avoid the fate of the poor animals that lay near but almost covered with the drifting snow. Night came and shut out the bleak desolation from our view but it did not still the howling winds that yet bellowed through the mountains bearing before them clouds of snow and beating against us cold and furious. It seemed that we were marked out for destruction and that the sun of another day might never rise to us. But He that rules the Storms willed it otherwise and the sun of the 27th rose clear uppon the gleaming peaks of the Mt St Joseph. I shall never forget the 26th of May 1827. Its incidents are engraven on my mind as well as the grateful feeling with which my heart was expanded when the storm was stilled.

On the 27th we resumed our journey N E 12 miles over the snow. The last fall of 15 inches in addition to what the horses sank in the old snow made the traveling verry fatigueing. Passing across a deep ravine and ascending a high point I could discover the plain. Thence N 13 miles the snow decreasing gradually until going down a high and steep hill it entirely disappeared and I came into a valley where there was some good grass. A valuable horse gave out and was left in the snow. I also lost my Pistol.[242]

---

[242] On this momentous day, Smith follows the headwaters of the Moke-

28th As my horses were much fatigued I lay by. The
general range of the Mountain at this place was about
N W & S E. My encampment was about 100 yards from
a high and steep bluff on the top of which at about 12
O Clock 10 or 12 indians showed themselves and raised
the accustomed yell but not succeeding in scaring us off
they collected a great many large rocks and being all
ready at once sent them down the hill at the same time
raising the yell. Finding that even this would not drive
us away they went off.[243]

29th N E 18 miles I left the water course on which
I was encamped running N W & passing over some
rocky hills came to and crossed a Creek coming from
the South East about 50 yards and running N W and
uniting about 6 miles below with the one on which I
had encamped. I surprised two squaws and was so close
to one of them that she could not well escape such an
expression of fear I had never before seen exhibited.
She ran towards me screaming and raising the stick
with which she had been digging roots in her whole
appearance realizing the Idea I had formed of a frantic

lumne (his "deep ravine") and still approximating the path of Route 4,
crosses the Sierra through Ebbetts Pass to add another distinction to his
remarkable accomplishments by becoming the first American to cross the range.
  He then turns north and begins the eastern descent by Kinney Creek and
presumably makes his camp on Silver Creek, in a valley now containing the
ruins of an old silver mine.
  [243] The stone-rolling Indians were Washoes, whose territory was in the
vicinity of Lake Tahoe and the Carson Valley east of the Sierra Nevada
(Kroeber, 569-73).

mother rushing to scare away some beast that would devour her child. wishing not to hurt her I avoided her formidable weapon and endeavored to pacify her but all in vain for when she went off her screams were still heard until lost in the distance. In the course of the day I saw some Antelope sign.[244]

30th   15 Miles East   crossed some high hills and came to a Stream 50 yds wide running N E. Crossed over and encamped on the East side. In this vicinity I saw some horse sign. On the N N E & E were ranges of high hills.[245]

------

[244] There is something of a problem in Smith's statement that he left the water course on which he encamped running "northwest," when, in fact, Silver Creek flows northeast. Otherwise it would seem that the group continues along Silver Creek or its adjacent hills until it meets the East Fork of the Carson River coming in from the southeast, and crosses what at that time of year could be considerable stream. Smith would then continue along the Carson until it turns northwest (possibly this is what he meant) after meeting Monitor Creek. He then turns to the northeast on Monitor Creek, and approximating present Route 89, heads toward the crossing of the mountains through Monitor Pass. No mention is made of the camp on the 29th; one can only assume by the distances mentioned on this and the next day that it was west of the pass itself.

It could possibly be argued from the first sentence in the day's entry that Smith left Silver Creek and headed directly east over the hills to the East Fork of the Carson, but this seems rather illogical.

[245] If our projected itinerary is correct, the trio continues on east through the hills on a course similar to that of Route 89 and enters Antelope Valley by way of Slinkard Creek. There in the valley they encounter the West Walker River running northeast.

Possibly Smith and his men continue on down the West Walker for a bit before camping; otherwise they could not have traveled the full fifteen miles. At any rate, they camp on the West Walker in Antelope Valley, surrounded on the north by the Pine Nut Mountains, and on the northeast and east by the Wellington Hills.

31st 16 miles East and encamped on a shallow creek 30 yds wide * (* in the course of this days travel I saw Salt of beautiful appearance that had lost its savor and was entirely tasteless.) running north. Some Antelopes were seen but verry wild.[246]

June 1st 22 Miles E S E   crossing a high range of hills running north & south I came to a lake extending from S E to N W supposed about 20 miles although its northerly limit was unknown and apparently about 8 miles broad.[247] As I was near the southern extremity of

[246] This day's entry is somewhat perplexing, for to get the Americans from the West Walker in Antelope Valley to the East Walker east of Cambridge Hills – points clearly at each end of the travel – requires more of a journey than the sixteen miles mentioned. And what route is used? Even the reference to salt is not specific enough to help. One suspects that rather than take the impractical course due east through the Wellington Hills the group continues on down the West Walker to about present Wellington and then cuts east through Smith Valley, over the hills north of Mount Etna near Mickey Canyon, into the Upper Mason Valley (Pine Grove Flat), and ultimately reaches the East Walker. There is, of course, the possibility that Smith follows the West Walker through Smith Valley and enters Monon Valley through Wilson Canyon; this, however, is a northeast course, not east, and would bring the party to the East Walker at a point so close to where it joins the western branch that the fact would probably have been noted. The attempt to reconstruct this day's journey is one of the more troublesome moments in this text.

[247] From wherever on the East Walker his camp was, Smith leads his men through Wheeler Pass and Cottonwood Creek, just north of Mount Grant, and brings them to the shores of Walker Lake to become the first Americans to gaze upon its waters. The party then continues the short distance to the southern end of the lake and encamps on its shores north of present Hawthorne.

The lake (as well as the river) was named by Frémont for his trapperscout and guide Joseph Walker. In November, 1845, coming west on his third California expedition, Frémont rendezvoused with Walker at the north end of the lake. The Smith and Frémont routes in Nevada are briefly identical from this camp of Smith's east to the eastern slope of the Toiyabe Range. See the

the Lake I went around in that direction in doing which I saw a considerable horse sign and seeing some indians at a Lodge I got close to them before they discovered that we were not indians they then immediately ran off. I took some fish that I found at the lodge and left some small presents in their rooms. I went on a little further where there was several families encamped. they were fishing with nets verry neatly made with fine meshes. I gave them some small presents they appeared verry friendly. I went 2 miles further and encamped near where three indians were fishing. I turned out my horses as usual and went to sleep. About ten O Clock at night I was awakened by the sound of horses feet. I started up and 20 or 30 horsemen rode by at full speed to where the fishermen were encamped. I awakened the men we collected our things together and made of them as good a breast work as we could and prepared ourselves for extremities. Presently 2 indians came as if to see if we were asleep. But finding we were awake they came close and sit down. I offered them some Tobacco but they would not take it. They returned to their companions and soon all came and surrounded us with their Bows strung and their arrows in their hands. They sat down and consulted with each other talking loud and harsh and frequently changing places some times all being on

"Map of Oregon and Upper California From the Surveys of John Charles Frémont And other Authorities drawn by Charles Preuss Under the Order of the Senate of the United States Washington City 1848," which is reproduced in Jackson and Spence in their map portfolio.

one side and then on the other. To the one that seemed
the principal character I offered some presents but he
would take nothing turning from me with disdain. If
my horses had been tied I should most certainly have
fired on them but as they were loose and as there was
a possibility that they might not commence I thought it
prudent not to be the agressor but to hold ourselves in
readiness to beat them off or sell our lives as dear as
possible. After about two hours they became peaceable
and made a fire. I then offered them some tobacco they
took it smoked and remained all night. It will be readily conjectured that I kept a verry close watch during
the remainder of the night. I do not know how to
account for the singular conduct of the indians. They
did not appear unanimous for the massacre and perhaps
saw our intention of making our scalps bear a good
price. we should not have fallen without some of them
in company.[248]

---

[248] Smith is, and will be for some time, among the Southern Paiutes, of
whom Frémont would offer the following description in 1845: "in this region
the condition of the Indian is nearly akin to that of the lower animals. Here
they are really *wild men*. In this wild state the Indian lives to get food. This
is his business. The superfluous part of his life, that portion which can be
otherwise employed, is devoted to some kind of warfare. From this lowest
condition, where he is found as the simplest element of existence, up to the
highest in which he is found on the continent, it is the same thing. In the
Great Basin, where nearly naked he travelled on foot and lived in the sage-
brush, I found him in the most elementary form; the men living alone; the
women living alone, but all after food. Sometimes one man cooking by his
solitary fire in the sage-brush which was his home, his bow and arrows and
bunch of squirrels by his side; sometimes on the shore of a lake or river
where food was more abundant a little bank of men might be found occupied

June 2d   In the morning they appeared friendly and told me that there was water to the East in the direction I wished to travel. I observed these indians had some Buffalo Robes knives and Spanish Blankets from which it appears they have some communication with the indians on Lewis's River and with the spanish indians. I moved on East about 20 miles and was obliged to encamp without water. The indians no doubt well knew there was no water and intended to deceive me and send me where I might perish for the want of it.[249]

3d   28 miles E N E   Having in that direction seen a snowy hill the day before I steered for it and just after night found water and encamped. In the course of the day a light shower of rain. Some Antelopes were seen but verry wild. One of my horses gave out and was left three miles back on the trail.[250]

---

in fishing; miles away a few women would be met gathering seeds and insects, or huddled up in a shelter of sagebrush to keep off the snow." (Jackson and Spence, II, 26-27.)

[249] For information about Smith's route through the remainder of Nevada, I am indebted again to Todd Berens. With instructions from Dale Morgan, and using this text, Berens and his wife explored the area in the summer of 1969 and provided valuable field comments which resolved several difficulties. The camps of June 2 through June 12 are those located by Berens.

On June 2, Smith, Gobel, and Evans move in an almost due east direction to make a dry camp at a spot in Soda Spring Valley about five miles northwest of present Luning (approximately 38°34′N, 118°16′W). Lewis's River is the Snake.

[250] This passage implies that, having seen the snowcapped height of Toiyabe Dome off in the distance, Smith uses it for a guide and leaves Soda Spring Valley, crossing northeast through the Gabbs Valley Range on a route

4th I sent back for the tired horse and had him brought up and then moved on N E 3 miles to a range of high hills running N and S & encamped.[251]

5th N E 15 miles over high ranges of hills bearing N & S.[252]

---

approximately that now used by Route 23. However, Berens questions whether the Dome would be visible from the valley: "We experienced low haze on the day we traveled through Soda Springs Valley, consequently our visibility was limited. But in spite of this fact, I doubt if Toiyabe Dome would be visible from the valley. The Cedar Mountains (T8N, R37E) block any view of the Shoshone or Toiyabe Ranges until the summit of the pass above Luning is reached. Perhaps on an exceptionally clear day, aided with some form of optical instrument, certain peaks of the two ranges might be visible from some point in the lower end of Soda Spring Valley. The reflection quality of snow would certainly enhance the possibility of sighting a distant point, but normally the peaks tend to blend together when seen from any great distance." (Berens to Dale Morgan, Sept. 22, 1969.)

At a point in T10N, R35E, where the highway crosses a dry wash, Smith's party turns east to follow the wash down into the Ione Valley. There they will find a small spring and camp in the wash at about 38°41′N, 117°52′W.

[251] The entry suggests that Smith continues on down the wash into Ione Valley, camping over near the base of the Shoshones, but still in the open valley at about 38°43′N, 117°43′W.

[252] It is apparent that the transcriber has made another one of his errors. Smith certainly would have gone on a southeast course and not attempted a northeast path which would have led him directly through the Shoshone and Toiyabe mountains. As Berens writes, ". . . one good look at the country on the other side of Luning convinced me that anyone experienced in overland travel would go around an obstacle rather than over it! . . From almost any point in Ione Valley, but especially from 'Luning Pass,' it would appear to even the most inexperienced traveler that it would be far easier to skirt the southern end of the Shoshone and Toiyabe Ranges than to attempt to make a direct assault on their ridge lines. It is my judgment that Smith's use of the plural 'ranges' is in reference to the crossing of the Shoshones in the vicinity of Willow Springs (just a trickle in August) and the Toiyabe in the vicinity

6th   E 12 miles then N E 6 miles and encamp on a creek running East.[253]

7th   E 15 miles crossing a plain and at the foot of a hill found water where I stopped for dinner. then crossing the range of hills and following an indian trail N 10 miles found water and good grass and encamped. saw an indian to day.[254]

8th   As my horses were much fatigued and the grass was tolerable good I concluded to rest. The general Character and appearance of the country I have passed is extremely Barren. High Rocky hills afford the only relief to the desolate waste for at the feet of these are found water and some vegetation While the intervals between are sand barren Plains.

9th   S S E 12 miles and finding it necessary to change

---

of Barrel and Mud Springs. . . The broad bench which separates the two points forms both a physical as well as a psychological break between the two ranges." (Berens to Morgan, Sept. 22, 1969.)

It would appear on the basis of projection, then, that Smith's camp was in the immediate vicinity of Cloverdale Ranch, but perhaps not as far east as Barrel or Mud Springs.

[253] Smith's travel on June 6 (although the distances as given are excessive) takes the three men down around the southern foot of the Toiyabe Range to an encampment at Peavine Creek (the Moore's Creek of the Frémont–Preuss map).

[254] Moving east across Big Smoky Valley, the trio probably stops for their midday meal just west of present Manhattan, and then crosses the southern tip of the Toquima Range directly east from Manhattan on a route approximating present Highway 69. Upon reaching the northern part of Ralston Valley, the group turns northeast to encamp for June 7 and 8 near what is now the abandoned site of Belmont.

my course to E N E I traveled 12 miles Leaving a high hill on the North and found a little spring in the plain by which I encamped. In the course of the day saw fresh sign of indians.[255]

10th   28 miles E   at 10 O Clock found the water and grass in the plain & stopped for the horses to eat. I there found an Indian and 2 squaws who had no opportunity of running away. I endeavored to talk a little with them by signs but found them too stupid or wilful. They had a piece of a Buffalo robe and a Beaver skin which last I bought of them – at 11 O Clock I continued my course E. Our remaining horses had now become so weak that we were general obliged to walk. At 3 O Clock one of them gave out and was left in the plain. Having crossed two Ranges of hills Just after dark I discovered a fire and steered towards it. and found an Indian Squaw and

---

[255] On June 9 the party travels southeast across Monitor Valley to take advantage of the McCann Canyon route through the Monitor Range. Smith then turns northeast up through Willow Creek Valley and, with the Monitor Range still to his north, moves on east through a break in the mountains. This cut, in the SE quadrant of T8N, R48E, where there is a primitive road today, leads to the head of Fish Lake Valley. There, at a spring (probably the headwaters of Hot Creek) at the head of the valley, the men make camp.

Berens made an attempt to cross the Monitor via McCann Canyon by jeep, "but lost the road at the summit. The pass is obvious from Belmont, gradual in approach, thinly timbered with juniper and cedar, and free of deep washes . . . the reverse slope is steep, but passable for mounted men. . . I gave up the search and made my way out of the canyon and turned north to cross the range at Barley Creek descending into the head of Willow Creek. On the basis of my experience, I would say that McCann Canyon and the unnamed pass used by the Barley Creek Road are the only two practical routes over this segment of the Monitor Range." (Berens to Morgan, Sept. 22, 1969.)

2 children who were of course much frightened. They appeared to be travelers having with them some water which they divided with us. I then for the first time saw scorpions prepared to eat. I went a short distance and encamped without water. During the night it rained which of course refreshed the horses.[256]

11th E 20 miles across a valley. Soon after starting I found a little water in some holes collected from the last rain. I encamped in a range of high hills where I found water. At that time we were on allowance of 4 ounces of dried meat per day and hardly the possibility of killing anything.[257]

12th 25 miles East Crossed over the range of hills on the top of which I found some Aspin and service

---

[256] From his camp, Smith moves on down Hot Creek Canyon and into Hot Creek Valley. Then moving slightly south of east, the group crosses the valley and enters the Pancake Range at about where U.S. Highway 6 does today. Moving along the highway route for two or three miles, the party camps at about 38°28′N, 116°06′W.

As Berens points out, "Smith's entry for June 10 failed to include a description of Hot Creek which, if for no other reason, should have been included because it is the first water that he would have encountered that flowed parallel to his course of travel. The creek is noticeably warm, its entire course abundantly supplied with pools of water, and had banks covered with grasses. Although it is hemmed in by steep walls, it offers easy passage to Hot Creek Valley to the east." (Berens to Morgan, *ibid.*) Possibly, though, Smith's reference to "water and grass in the plain" has some connection with Hot Creek.

[257] On this day, Smith parallels the course of Highway 6 and proceeds east through a valley within the Pancake Range and transits Black Rock Summit to camp on the east slope of the range. Here, near present Big Spring, the mountains would rise to nearly 3,000 feet behind him, thus satisfying the description of "high hills."

Bushes. then crossing a valley I found a little water and encamped but without grass. In the course of the day I killed a hare. I mention this for in this country game is so scarce and wild that it is a most hopeless task to kill anything. An Antelope or Black tailed deer may sometimes be seen solitary and wild as the wind.[258]

13th   E 15 miles crossed a plain and another range of hills high and Rocky finding no water and observing a smoke to the North I traveled in that direction 15 miles and found water and grass and encamped. In the course of the day I saw several Antelopes but could not get a shot and in the evening an Indian but he ran off.[259]

14th   North 8 miles along a wet piece of ground on the E side of which I encamped. My horses were so much reduced that it was necessary to give them rest and for this reason I made a short days travel.[260]

---

[258] The trio continues east across Railroad Valley, turning away from the path of Highway 6 at a point which brings them to approximately present Blue Eagle Spring (or slightly north). They then enter the Grant Range by Johnson Canyon south of Ragged Ridge, and come to rest in the high valley which separates the northern Grant Range from the southern edge of Horse Range.

[259] Continuing east across the narrow plain, Smith and his party cross down past Wells Station at the southern end of the Horse Mountains and into White River Valley. Seeing smoke farther to the north (more likely to the northeast), the travelers move up the valley in the direction of Indian Springs, possibly getting that far for their camp.

[260] Traveling on north a few miles, the group moves up along ground made wet by the various small tributaries of the White River. They make camp at a spot perhaps three miles south of present Lund.

15th   N E 10 miles and encamped at the head of the springs which forms the wet ravine on which I had made my last two encampments.[261]

16th   I lay by to rest. for 12 days I have been with my two men on an allowance of   ounces of dried meat per day and the last of it was eat for supper last night. No possibility of killing any game. My horses extremely poor and one so lame in his hind feet as to be unable to travel. He was shod before but his hind feet were worn to the quick. As a last resource for provision I determined to kill this horse and dry some of the best of his meat. Accordingly in the morning I had him killed. It was bad eating but we were hungry enough to eat almost any thing.

17th   E N E 30 miles crossing 2 ranges of Rocky hills and the intervening valleys and encamp in a 3d range of hills without water having seen none since morning.[262]

---

[261] The day's travel on June 15, as projected in this analysis, brings Smith's party to the head of White River Valley, not far distant from the mouth of Water Canyon.

[262] Having somewhat recruited the horses and his men, Smith turns east to move up Water Canyon and across the Egan Range.

The day's entry is another perplexing one in that it does not seem to adhere very closely to the actual topography of the area through which Smith passes. In fact, the discrepancies were disturbing enough to suggest that the proposed route was incorrect; yet what comes immediately before, and what immediately follows, fit so well into an over-all projection that one is inclined to make some exceptions here. The problem centers on the "2 ranges of Rocky Hills and the intervening valleys" which is a somewhat exaggerated view of crossing the Egans at this point. Perhaps by a stretch of the imagination, it might satisfy the requirement.

Proceeding beyond this puzzle, however, the party's route takes them across

18th E 10 miles starting early I crossed the chain on whic[h I] was encamped but seeing no prospect of water Eastwardly I turned N E and after traveling 10 miles I fell in with some indians 14 in number. we were the[n] close to water which happened verry well for one of my men had stoped a short distance back being able to proceed no further. The Indians went with me to the spring and I sent one of them with a little kettle of water to the man that was left behind. After drinking he was sufficiently refreshed to come up. The Indians gave me two small ground squirrels which we found somewhat better than the horse meat. They likewise showed me a kind of water rush which they ate. I tasted of it and found it pleasant I had three horns for the purpose of carrying water. In these sandy plains we filled them at every opportunity But I seldom drank more than half a pint before they were exhausted for neither of my men could do as well without water as myself.[263]

19th 15 miles N E as a high range of hills lay on the East I was obliged to travel N E to a low gape in

---

Steptoe Valley to a camp in a third range, the Schell Creek Mountains, near Connors Canyon where the highway runs today.

[263] Crossing over the Schell Creek Range by means of Connors Canyon, the party emerges into Spring Valley near present Majors Place, and in the attempt to move east through the valley, Robert Evans (it must be he, for he falters again in the Utah desert on June 25, and does not elect to return to the West Coast on Smith's second expedition) collapses. It is apparently at Willard Spring, or perhaps even at Layton Spring farther north, that Smith and Gobel locate water with the help of their Indian friends.

the chain and then crossing over encamped on the East side we there found some onions which made the horse meat relish much better.[264]

20th   N E 20 miles along a valley sandy as usual and just at night found water. In this part of the plain almost all the high hills have snow on their tops. But for these snowy Peaks the country would be utterly impassible as they furnish almost the only grass or water of this unhospitable land. They are to this plain like the islands of the Ocean. Rising but a short distance from the sandy base the snowy region commences which is an evidence of the great elevation of this plain.

[The]re after encamping some Indians came to me. They appeared verry friendly. These as well as those last mentioned I supposed were somewhat acquainted with whites as I saw among them some Iron arrow points and some Beads. They gave me some squirrels and in return I gave them presents of such little things as I had after which they went to their camp and we our rest.[265]

21st   25 miles North. Early this morning the indians

---

[264] Keeping the Snake Mountains and towering Wheeler Peak to the east, the group moves on up to cross the range through Sacramento Pass, the cut now used by highways 6 and 50. They then descend on the east to make camp at a spot near the present Nevada-Utah border.

[265] Now going north along the east side of the Snake Range, Smith's party makes camp on one of the several streams running down from the mountains into Snake Valley. It could possibly be Hampton Creek, for the distance Smith allows for this day's travel and the next seem excessive when compared with the actual mileage.

that were at the camp last night returned and with them
several others. They seemed to have come out of mere
curiosity and as I was ready for starting they accompanied me a short distance. Some of them I presume
had never before seen a white man and as they were
handling and examining almost every thing I fired off
my gun as one of them was fingering about the double
triggers. At the sound some fell flat on the ground and
some sought safety in flight. The indian who had hold
of the gun alone stood still although he appeared at first
thunder struck yet on finding that he was not hurt he
called out to his companions to return. I endeavored to
learn from those indians by signs something in relation
to the distance and course to the Salt Lake But from
them I could get no satisfaction whatever for instead
of answering my signs they would imitate them as
nearly as possible. After vexing myself for some time
with those children of nature I left them and continued
on my way. All the indians I had seen since leaving the
Lake had been the same unintelligent kind of beings.
Nearly naked having at most a scanty robe formed from
the skin of the hare peculiar to this plain which is cut
into narrow strips and interwover with a kind of twine
or cord made apparently from wild flax or hemp. They
form a connecting link between the animal and intelec-
tual creation and quite in keeping with the country in
which they are located. In the course of the day I passed
water several times. It came out from a range of hills

on the west on the top of which was some snow. I encamped on the bank of a Salt Lake.[266] The water was
verry salt and a good deal of salt was formed along the
beach. In crossing a mirey place just before encamping
one of my horses was mired. After some considerable
exertion I found it impossible to get him out   I therefore killed him and took a quarter of his flesh which
was a seasonable replenishment for our stock of provision as the little I took of the horse I killed last was
at that time exhausted.

22nd June 1827[267]   North 25 Miles. My course was

---

[266] For the final entry in this particular section of the journal, Smith de-
scribed his arrival at Salt Marsh Lake, just east of present Gandy, Utah.
Generally, through this section of Utah, the Indians Smith meets will be
Gosiutes (or Goshutes), a Shoshone connection, and this description recalls
some observations made by Thomas J. Farnham in 1843 of other Gosiutes in
Skull Valley: "They wear no clothing of any description – build no shelter.
They eat roots, lizards, and snails . . . And when the lizard and snail
and wild roots are buried in the snows in winter, they . . . dig holes
. . . and sleep and fast till the weather permits them to go abroad again
for food . . . These poor creatures are hunted in the spring of the year,
when weak and helpless . . . and when taken, are fattened, carried to
Santa Fe and sold as slaves." (As quoted in the American Guide Series, *Utah,
A Guide to the State,* 385.)

[267] The text for the balance of the trip back to the Rendezvous is from the
section of Smith's journal discovered and published by Maurice Sullivan in
his *Travels* in 1934 on pages 19-26. It is here reproduced through the kind
permission of the present owner of the manuscript: The Jennewein Western
Collection, Dakota Wesleyan University, Mitchell, S.D.

The present version of the text was made from a microfilm in the possession
of the Missouri Historical Society. For Dale Morgan's interpretation of Smith's
route through Utah – one which seems perfectly valid – *see* Morgan, *Smith,*
211-15. With some slight modifications, it is essentially the itinerary offered
here.

parallel with a chain of hills on the west on the tops of which was some snow and from which ran a creek to the north east. On this creek I encamped. The Country in the vicinity so much resembled that on the south side of the Salt Lake that for a while I was induced to believe that I was near that place. During the day I saw a good many Antelope but could not kill any. I however killed 2 hares which when cooked at night we found much better than horse meat.[268]

June 23d N E 35 Miles. Moving on in the morning I kept down the creek on which we had encamped until it was lost in a small Lake. We then filled our horns and continued on our course, passing some brackish as well as some verry salt springs and leaving on the north of the latter part of the days travel a considerable Salt Plain. Just before night I found water that was drinkable but continued on in hopes of find better and was obliged to encamp without any.[269]

June 24th N E 40 Miles I started verry early in hopes of soon finding water. But ascending a high point

---

[268] Keeping the Deep Creek Mountains, which now replace the Snake Range on their left, the group moves north to camp on Thomas Creek, which runs northeast from the mountains (*see* Sullivan, *Travels*, 165 n.37).

[269] Thomas Creek today is considerably less impressive than in Smith's time and the small lake has disappeared. The trio, however, moves northeast past the northern tip of the Fish Springs Range, passes the brackish salt springs near present Wilson Health Springs (or perhaps the Fish Springs themselves), and then enters the southern tip of the Great Salt Lake Desert, the present Wendover Bombing and Gunnry Range. They make camp at some unspecified point west and south of the Dugway Range.

of a hill I could discover nothing but sandy plains or dry Rocky hills with the Exception of a snowy mountain off to the N E at the distance of 50 or 60 Miles. When I came down I durst not tell my men of the desolate prospect ahead. but framed my story so as to discourage them as little as possible. I told them I saw something black at a distance near which no doubt we would find water. While I had been up on the one of the horses gave out and had been left a short distance behind. I sent the men back to take the best of his flesh for our supply was again nearly exhausted whilst I would push forward in search of water. I went on a short distance and waited until they came up. They were much discouraged with the gloomy prospect but I said all I could to enliven their hopes and told them in all probability we would soon find water. But the view ahead was almost hopeless. With our best exertion we pushed forward walking as we had been for a long time over the soft sand. That kind of traveling is verry tiresome to men in good health who can eat when and what they choose and drink as often as they desire. and to us worn down with hunger and fatigue and burning with thirst increased by the blazing sands it was almost insurportable. At about 4 O Clock we were obliged to stop on the side of a sand hill under the shade of a small Cedar. We dug holes in the sand and laid down in them for the purpose of cooling our heated bodies. After resting about an hour we resumed our wearysome journey and traveled until 10 O Clock at night when we laid down to take a little repose. Previous to this and a short time after sun down I saw several turtle doves and as I did not recollect of ever having seen them more than 2 or 3 miles from water I spent more than a hour in looking for water but it was in vain. Our sleep was not repose for tormented nature made us dream of things we had not and for the want of which it then seemed possible and even probable we might perish in the desert unheard of and unpitied. In those moments how trifling were all those things that hold such an absolute sway over the busy and the prosperous world. My dreams were not of Gold or ambitious honors but of my distant quiet home of murmuring brooks of cooling cascades. After a short rest we continued our march and traveled all night. The murmur of falling waters still sounding in our ears and the apprehension that we might never live to hear that sound in reality weighed heavily uppon us.[270]

---

[270] Tired as the men are, the party now embarks on some of the most difficult and discouraging travel of the entire expedition. Moving up to pass between the Dugway Range on the south and Granite Peak on the north, Smith ascends a hill (possibly either the Dugways or Sapphire Mountain) and is presented with the bleak view across what is now the Dugway Proving Grounds. The only relief is the sight of the Stansbury Range (and perhaps some of the Onaqui Mountains) far off in the distance.

After passing Granite Peak, Smith journeys among the sand dunes in the approximate direction of what is now the Stark Road. Someplace in that desert, he and his men rest briefly and see the doves. Charles Kelly in his *Salt Desert Trails, 25,* mentions that there is a spring at Granite Peak, which Smith misses, or perhaps the doves found their water on Government Creek to the east. Certainly it would appear that the party camps someplace along

June 25th   When morning came it saw us in the same unhappy situation pursuing our journey over the desolate waste now gleming in the sun and more insuportably tormenting than it had been during the night. At 10 O Clock Robert Evans laid down in the plain under the shade of a small cedar being able to proceed no further. The Mountain of which I have before spoken was apparently not far off and we left him and proceeded onward in the hope of finding water in time to return with some in season to save his life. After traveling about three Miles we came to the foot of the Mt and then to our inexpressible joy we found water. Goble plunged into it at once and I could hardly wait to bath my burning forehead before I was pouring it down regardless of the consequences. Just before we arrived at the spring I saw two indians traveling in the direction in which Evans was left and soon after the report of two guns was heard in quick succession. This considerably increased our apprehension for his safety but shortly after a smoke was seen back on the trail and I took a small kettle of water and some meat and going back found him safe. he had not seen the indians and had discharged his gun to direct me where he lay and for the same purpose had raised a smoke. He was indeed far gone being scarcely able to speak. When I came

---

the southern end of the Cedar Mountains (near either Little Dove or Little Granite mountains), somewhere west of present Dugway. There is nothing to indicate that they get as far as Skull Valley itself, as Morgan suggests (Morgan, *Smith,* 418 n.42).

the first question he asked me was have you any water! I told him I had plenty and handed the kettle which would hold 6 or 7 quarts in which there was some meat mixed with the water. O says he why did you bring the meat and putting the kettle to his mouth he did not take it away untile he had drank all the water of which there was at least 4 or 5 quarts and then asked me why I had not brought more. This however revived him so much that he was able to go on to the spring. I cut the horse meat and spread it out to dry and determined to remain for the rest of the day that we might repose our wearied and emaciated bodies. I have at different times suffered all the extremes of hunger and thirst. Hard as it is to bear for succesive days the knawings of hunger yet it is light in comparison to the agony of burning thirst, and [o]n the other hand I have observed that a man reduced by hunger is some days in recovering his strength. A man equally reduced by thirst seems renovated almost instantaneneously. Hunger can be endured more than twice as long as thirst. To some it may appear surprising that a man who has been for several days without eating has a most incessant desire to drink and although he can drink but a little at a time yet he wants it much oftener than in ordinary circumstances. In the course of the day several indians showed themselves on the high points of the hills but would not come to my camp.[271]

---

[271] From the very general description given, it would appear that Robert Evans gave out near the entrance to Skull Valley, perhaps not far from pres-

26th June   N 10 miles along a valley and encamped at some brackish water having passed during the day several salt springs and one Indian Lodge. The lodge was occupied by 2 indians one squaw and 2 children. They were somewhat alarmed but friendly and when we made signs to them of being hungry they cheerfully divided with us some antelope meat. They spoke like the snake Indians and by enquiry I found they were Panakhies from Lewis's River. They had some pieces of Buffalo Robes and told me that a few days travel to the North E. Buffalo were plenty. Although they knew the shoshones I could not learn any thing from them in relation to the Salt Lake. In the evening I discovered from a high piece of ground what appeared to be a large body of water.[272]

---

ent Dugway. Smith and Gobel then continue their march to an undetermined spring at the foot of the Stansbury or Onaqui mountains where they find the water which averts tragedy. Morgan offers that the water was found at Spring Creek, just inside the present Skull Valley Indians Reservation (Morgan, *Smith,* 418 n.43), which is also a strong possibility.

The group seems to have advanced some distance up the valley, and probably stops in the vicinity of the Indian reservation. Sullivan, *Travels,* 166 n.42, relates that "Charles Kelly . . . tells me that Moodywoc, an ancient Goshute Indian, recalls hearing his grandmother say that in her girlhood three starving men, the first whites she had ever seen, emerged from the Salt Desert." Kelly in his *Salt Desert Trails,* 25, has another variant, which he quotes from Isaac K. Russell's, *Hidden Heroes of the Rockies:* "For years after Smith's journey the Piute Indians of Skull Valley, Utah, repeated the tradition that the first white men they ever saw were three who staggered, almost naked, in from the western desert, and were half crazy from breathing alkali dust." *See also* the story mentioned earlier in note 252.

[272] Travel ten miles north from their camp of June 25 would put Smith and his party in the general vicinity of Horseshoe Springs. Sullivan, *Travels,*

June 27th   North 10 Miles along a valley in which were many salt springs. Coming to the point of the ridge which formed the Eastern boundary of the valley I saw an expanse of water Extending far to the North and East. The Salt Lake a joyful sight was spread before us. Is it possible said the companions of my sufferings that we are so near the end of our troubles. For myself I durst scarcely believe that it was really the Big Salt Lake that I saw. It was indeed a most cheering view for although we were some distance from the depo yet we knew we would soon be in a country where we would find game and water which were to us objects of the greatest importance and those which would contribute more than any others to our comfort and happiness. Those who may chance to read this at a distance from the scene may perhaps be surprised that the sight of this lake surrounded by a wilderness of more than 2000 miles diameter excited in me these feelings known to the traveler who after long and perilous journeying comes again in view of his home. But so it was with me for I had traveled so much in the vicinity of the Salt Lake that it had become my home of the wilderness. After coming in view of the lake I traveled East keeping nearly paralel with the shore of the lake. At about 25 miles from my last encampment I found a spring of fresh water and encamped. The water during

---

166 n.41 correctly identifies the Indians as Bannocks, a Shoshonean tribe from the Snake River.

the day had been generally Salt. I saw several antelope but could not get a shot at them.[273]

28th   East 20 miles   traveling nearly parallel with the shore of the Lake. When I got within a mile of the outlet of the Uta Lake which comes in from the south East I found the ground which is thick covered with flags and Bulrushes overflowed to a considerable distance from the channel and before I got to the current the water had increased to between 2 & 3 feet and the cain grass and Bulrushes were extremely thick. The channel was deep and as the river was high was of course rapid and about 60 yards wide. As I would have to wade a long distance should I attempt to return before I would find dry land I determined to make a raft and for this purpose cut a quantity of Cain Grass for of this material there was no want. The grass I tied into Bundles and attaching them together soon formed a raft sufficiently strong to bear my things. In the first place I swam and lead my horse over the mule following to the opposite bank which was also overflowed. I then returned and attaching a cord to the raft and holding the end in my mouth I swam before the raft while the two men swam behind. Unfortunately neither of my men were good swimmers and the current being strong we were swept down a considerable distance and it was with great

---

[273] On this encouraging day, Smith travels to the northern tip of the Stansbury Mountains from which spot he catches sight of his "home in the wilderness," the Great Salt Lake. The party then continues eastwardly along the shore to camp near present Marshall in the Tooele Valley.

difficulty that I was enabled to reach the shore as I was verry much strangled. When I got to the shore I put my things on the mule and horse and endeavored to go out to dry land but the animals mired and I was obliged to leave my things in the water for the night and wade out to the dry land. We made a fire of sedge and after eating a little horse flesh we laid down to rest.[274]

29th   15 Miles North   Early in the morning I brought my things out from the water and spread them out to dry. We were verry weak and worn down with suffering and fatigue but we thought ourselves near the termination of our troubles for it was not more than four days travel to the place where we expected to find my partners. At 10 O Clock we moved onward and after traveling 15 miles encamped. Just before encamping I got a shot at a Bear and wounded him badly but did not kill him. At supper we ate the last of our horse meat and talked a little of the probability of our suffering being soon at an end. I say we talked a little for men suffering from hunger never talk much but rather bear their sorrows in moody silence which is much preferable to fruitless compaint.[275]

---

274 Smith's course around the southern shore of the lake eventually brings him to another familiar landmark, the Jordan River, which in its swollen condition offers a considerable challenge.

275 The group now moves north along the route they had used coming south in the previous August. In three days (June 29, 30, and July 1) they cross the Weber River (although Smith does not mention it) and come to the site of present Brigham City, at the mouth of Box Elder Creek.

30th   North 15 miles. I Started early and as Deer were tolerably plenty I went on ahead and about 8 O Clock got a shot at a Deer. he ran off I followed him and found a good deal of blood and told the men to stop while I should look for him. I soon found him laying in a thicket. As he appeared nearly dead I went up to him took hold of his horns when he sprang up and ran off. I was vexed at myself for not shooting him again when it was in my power and my men were quite discouraged. However I followed on and in a short time found him again. I then made sure of him by cutting his ham strings It was a fine fat Buck and it was not long before we struck up a fire and had some of his meat cooking. We then employed ourselves most pleasantly in eating for about two hours and for the time being forgot that we were not the happiest people in the world or at least thought but of our feast that was eaten with a relish unknown to a palace. So much do we make our estimation of happiness by a contrast with our situation that we were as much pleased and as well satisfied with our fat venison on the bank of the Salt Lake as we would have been in the possession of all the Luxuries and enjoyments of civilized life in other circumstances. These things may perhaps appear trifling to most readers but let any one of them travel over the same plain as I did and they will consider the killing of a buck a great achievement and certainly a verry useful one. After finishing our repast the meat of the Deer was cut and dried over the fire.

July 1st   25 miles North along the shore of the Lake. Nothing material occured.

2nd   20 Miles North East made our way to the Cache. But just before arriving there I saw some indians on the opposite side of a creek. It was hardly worth while as I thought to be any wise careful so I went directly to them and found as near as I could judge by what I knew of the language to be a band of the snakes. I learned from them that the whites as they term our parties were all assembled at the little Lake a distance of about 25 miles. There was in this camp about 200 Lodges of indians and as the[y] were on their way to the rendezvous I encamped with them.[276]

3d   I hired a horse and a guide and at three O Clock arrived at the rendezvous   My arrival caused a considerable bustle in camp for myself and party had been given up as lost. A small Cannon brought up from St Louis was loaded and fired for a salute.[277]

---

[276] *See* note 17. There seems no reason to doubt that Smith returns to the cache on Blacksmith Creek in Cache Valley by reversing the route he used in leaving, going up Box Elder Canyon and then through Sardine Canyon. At the cache, Smith learns that the Rendezvous is assembled at Bear Lake.

[277] Apparently leaving the cache by way of Blacksmith Creek Canyon, Smith and his Indian guide move on east to the Rendezvous at the southern end of Bear Lake near present Laketown (Morgan, *Smith,* 215, 228).

Harrison G. Rogers
Daybook I

Introduction

The original manuscript of the Harrison Rogers daybook, as Harrison Dale first noted, has endured a remarkable history. Taken by the Indians along with other belongings of Rogers after his murder in the Umpqua massacre in Oregon on July 14, 1828, the papers were recovered from the Umpqua in the fall of 1828 by Jedediah Smith, who brought them back to St. Louis in 1830. After Smith's death the next year, Rogers' journals came into General Ashley's possession, and eventually passed to Mrs. Benjamin F. Gray whose mother had been Ashley's stepdaughter. Mrs. Gray presented the papers to the Missouri Historical Society early in this century.

The Rogers daybook is written on two distinct types of paper. The first segment is on six pages of machine-made paper measuring approximately 12¾ by 7¾ inches and bearing no watermark. The pages are folded lengthwise and were once sewn in an informal fashion along the crease. This portion contains ledger entries (most of which are published here for the first time) and a narrative which begins abruptly in the middle of what must have been an entry for November 26, 1826, and breaks off in the middle of a sentence in the entry for December 20. In general, the ledger accounts form the first portion of this fragment and the narrative passages are toward the end; but that states the case too simply, for entries often seem at random and sometimes lack chronological continuity. The abrupt start and finish of the narrative portion suggests, as others have also surmised, that these are the pages surviving after part of Rogers' daybook was turned over, along with Smith's notes, to Governor Echeandia in San Diego for transmittal to Mexican authorities.

The second segment of daybook 1 consists of four pages of hand-laid paper bearing Spanish watermarks and measuring approximately 12¼ by 8½ inches. The physical arrangement of the contents, which cover the period from January 1-27, 1827, is even more perplexing than that of the first portion, and it is impossible to reconstruct any logical relation of the pages, one to another, as they might have existed originally. These sheets are also folded lengthwise and were apparently joined together along the seam in some fashion at one time. One assumes that Rogers obtained the paper at San Gabriel.

Any reconstruction of the order of material in the daybook must be somewhat arbitrary in certain passages, and the entries are presented here in a way which will establish a chronological continuity for the reader. However, style, spelling, and punctuation have been left as near as possible to what appears on the original pages. The text could have been "tidied up" – Dale did so in his version – but that degree of editing destroys something of the flavor of Rogers' personality, and the immediacy of the entries is lost. Further, this version has been annotated only to the extent that such remarks amplify what Dale has already done, or clarify dates and proper names that also appear in the Smith journal.

The Accounts

MEMORANDUM OF MERCHANDISE TAKEN BY J. S. SMITH FOR THE SOUTH WEST EXPEDITION

August 15th 1826

4 dozen B. knives
1 Paper Tax.   2 lbs Beads
1½ dozen looking Glasses
2, 3 pt Am. Blanketts
3, 2½ pt "   Blanketts
1 Read Shawl
70 lbs Lead
55 lbs Powder   55 lbs Tobacco
6 Frenchen chissels
1 Fuzie

| John Gaiter | —— | Dr | |
| To 1 wipeing stick | | | $1.50 |

| Daniel Fugerson | | Dr | |
| To 1 wipeing stick | | | $1.50 |

| H. G. Rogers | | Dr | |
| To 1 wipeing stick | | | $1.50 |

J. S. Smith	——	Dr
To 1½ lbs hard soap		
To 3 cakes chaving soap		

| Daniel Fugerson | | Dr | |
| To 2 cakes shaving soap | | | $1.00 |

| Abraham Laplant | | Dr | |
| To soap   150 cts | | | $1.50 |

| Reubaseau | —— | Dr | |
| To soap   150 cts | | | $1.50 |

| Reubaseau | —— | Dr |
| To 1 Trap spring | | |

| J. S. Smith | | Dr | |
| To 1 wipeing stick | | | $1.50 |

| Martin McCoy | | Dr | |
| To 2,00 cts for P. Ranne } | | | $2.00 |

Peter Ranne	Cr	August 15th 1826	
By McCoy	$2.00	Abraham Laplant	Dr
		To 2 Cups Coffee	$4.00
Reubaseau	Dr		
To 1 Pint Rum	$3.00	Harrison G. Rogers	Dr
		To 4 cups coffee	$8.00
Neppasang	Dr	To 3 do sugar	$6.00
To 1 Pint Rum	$3.00		
		Arthur Black	Dr
Robert Evans	Dr	To ½ cup sugar }	
To 1 Pint Rum	$3.00	for P. Ranne }	$1.00
Arthur Black	Dr		
To 1 Pint Rum	$3.00	Stephen Terry [1]	Dr
		To 1.25 cents worth }	
A. Laplant	Dr	of merchandise }	$1.25
To ½ Pint Rum	$1.50	for Danl Ferguson }	
John Hannah	Dr	Arthur Black	Dr
To ½ Pint Rum	$1.50	To ½ cup Tea	
		" ¼ sugar	
Martin McCoy	Dr		
To 1 Gill Rum 75/100	$0.75	Robert Evans	Dr
		To ½ Cup Tea	
Manuel Lazarus	Dr	" ¼ do sugar	
To ½ Pint Rum	$1.50		
Manuel Eustavan	Dr	Manuel Eustavan	Dr
To ½ Pint Rum	$1.50	To 1 Sirsingle 300 cts	$3.00
Peter Ranne	Dr	Manuel Eustavan	Cr
To ½ Pint Rum	$1.50	By 1 Beaver skin	$3.00

[1] Stephen Terry appears in General Ashley's account ledger for the July, 1825, Rendezvous (Ashley Papers, MHS), but apparently is otherwise unmentioned in fur trade documents. The 1830 census lists a Stephen Terry, between 30 and 40 years of age, in St. Louis (Morgan, *Ashley*, 294 n.233).

James Read	Cr
By 1 Otter skin	$2.00

Daniel Ferguson	Dr
To 1 wipeing stick	$1.50

Martin McCoy	Dr
To 2 dollars worth merchandise for P. Ranne	
P. Ranne	Cr
By McCoy	$2.00

August 15th 1826

Daniel Fugerson	Dr
To ½ Cup Powder	
To ½ lb Lead	

Manuel Eustavan	Dr
To ½ cup Powder ¾ lb lead	

Robert Evans	Dr
Has on hand Powder and lead	

James Read has on hand
Powder and lead ——

John Gaiter	
To ½ Cup Powder ½ lb lead	

Arthur Black has Powder
and lead on hand ——

August 16th 1826

H. G. Rogers	Dr
To ½ Pint Rum ——	$1.50

James Reed	Dr
To ½ Pint Rum	$1.50

John Wilson	Dr
To ½ Pint Rum	$1.50

Robert Evans	Dr
To ½ Pint Rum	$1.50

Neppasang	Dr
To 1 Gill Rum 75/100	$0.75

Reubaseau	Dr
To 1 Gill Rum 75/100	$0.75

James Read	Dr
To 1 Gill Rum 75/100	$0.75

Emanuel Lazarus	Dr
To 1 lb Tobacco 150 cts	$1.50

James Reed	Dr
To 1 lb Tobacco 150 cts	$1.50

Arthur Black	Dr
To 1 lb Tobacco 150 cts	$1.50

John Wilson	Dr
To 1 lb Tobacco 150 cts	$1.50

John Gaiter	Dr
To 1 lb Tobacco 150 cts	$1.50

John Hannah	Dr
To 1 lb Tobacco 150 cts	$1.50

Manuel Eustavan	Dr
To 1 lb Tobacco 150 cts	$1.50

August 16th   1826

Daniel Fugerson	Dr	
To 1 lb Tobacco	150 cts	$1.50

Harrison G. Rogers	Dr	
To 1 lb Tobacco	150 cts	$1.50

Abraham Laplant	Dr	
To 1 lb Tobacco	150 cts	$1.50

18th

Reubaseau	Dr	
To shewing one horse		$5.00

Merchandise presented to the Eutaw Indians by J. S. Smith, August 22nd 1826.
3 yards Red Ribbon, 10 awls, 1 Razor 1 durk knife, 1 brass handle knife, 1 lb Powder, 40 Balls, arrow points, ½ lb Tobacco ——

August 23rd   1826

Emanuel Lazarus	Dr	
To 1 Wilson knife		$1.50

H. G. Rogers	Dr	
To ¼ oz. Bucks ——		

(24th)

Emanuel Eustavan	Dr	
To 1 pr Spurs 600 cts		$6.00

John Hannah	Dr	
To 1 Wilkinson knife		$1.50

August 27th   1826

Indian presents   1 Tin Kettle, 3 yards Red Strouding, 4 Razors, 2 durk knives, 2 Butcher knives, 50 Balls   1 lb Powder, 3 looking Glasses, 2 dozen Rings, 1 dozen combs   4 hawk Bills, 2 stretching needles, 2 doz. awls, Buttons 1 large green handle knife

August 28th   1826

Silas Gobel	Dr	
To balance on Deer skin		$1.00

Manuel Eustavan	Dr	
To 1½ yards Red Stroud		$15.00
To 2 awls ——		
To 1 looking Glass ——		
To 1 2½ point Blankett		$12.00

30th

James Read	Dr	
To 1 Wilkinson knife		$1.50

Manuel Eustavan	Dr	
To 1 Black Silk hand.		$3.00

30th

J. S. Smith	Cr
By 1 U.S. Pistol	
In exchange for a horn	

September 1st   1826

Neppasang	Dr	
To exchange in Riffles		$

Manuel Eustavan	Dr	
To 1 lb Tobacco	$1.50	

Silas Gobel	Dr
To ½ lb Tobacco	

September 6th   1826

Silas Gobel	Dr
To 1 knife 150 cts	$1.50
To 1 Spear 350 cts	$3.50

September 8th   1826

Arthur Black	Dr
To 1 Gun lock	$8.00
To 1 Trigger	1.00

Manuel Eustavan	Dr
To 2 Knives @	
150 cts pr knife	$3.00
To 1 mockason awl	1.00

James Reed	Dr
To 1 Knife 150 cts	$1.50

Indian present   1 Small Green
handle Knife

September 21st   1826

James Reed	Dr
To his assumption for	
A. Laplant	$10.00

21st

Abraham Laplant	Cr
By James Reed	$10.00

21st

John Hannah	Cr
By 1 wiper Stick for } J. S. Smith	$1.50

John Gaiter	Dr
To 1 pair sheep skin leggins	$1.50
To 1 Deer Skin	$1.25

James Reed	Dr
To 1 Deer Skin	$1.25

Silas Gobel	Dr
To 2 skins	$2.00

22nd

Robert Evans	Dr
To 2 dressed skins @ 87½ /100 pr skin	$1.75

Martin McCoy	Dr
To 2 dressed skins @ 87½ /100 pr skin	$1.75

Reubaseau	Dr
To 1 Beaver chissel & spear	

Neppasang	Dr
To 1 Beaver chissel & spear	

September 23rd   1826

Arthur Black	Dr
To 1 Knife	$1.50

Silas Gobel	Dr
To 1 Knife	$1.50

Daniel Ferguson   Dr
To 1 Knife $1.50

24th

Silas Gobel   Dr
To 1 Dressed Deer skin
75/100 $0.75

28th

Silas Gobel   Dr
To 1 mockason awl

Muddy River   Octr 1st   1826
John Wilson   Dr
To 1 lb Tobacco   150 cts $1.50

John Hannah   Dr
To 1 lb Tobacco   150 cts $1.50

James Reed   Dr
To 1½ lbs Tobacco 225 cts $2.25

Manuel Lazarus   Dr
To 1½ lbs Tobacco 225 cts $2.25

Daniel Ferguson   Dr
To ¾ lb Tobacco
112½ cts $1.12½

Manuel Lazarus   Dr
To ½ lb   75 cts $0.75

Silas Gobel   Dr
To ½ lb Tobacco   75 cts $0.75

Harrison G. Rogers   Dr
To 1 lb Tobacco   150 cts $1.50

Abraham Laplant   Dr
To 1 lb Tobacco   150 cts $1.50

Muddy River   Oct. 2nd   1826
Harrison G. Rogers   Dr
To 2 sheep skins $2.50

Arthur Black   Dr
To 1 sheep skin $1.50

Siskadee   Octr 5th   1826
Silas Gobel   Cr
By 1 Tin striker   300 cts $3.00

J. S. Smith   Dr
To his assumption for S.
Gobel for Tin striker $3.00

Siskady   Octr 24th   1826
Silas Gobel   Dr
To 1 knife   150 cts $1.50

Arthur Black   Dr
To 1 knife   150 cts $1.50

Daniel Ferguson   Dr
To 1 knife   150 cts $1.50

John Wilson   Dr
To 1 knife   150 cts $1.50

Abraham Laplant   Cr
By difference in Breach
Cloths   250 cts ——— $2.50

Siskadee   November 5th   1826
John Gaiter   Dr
To 1 Awl   25/100 $0.25

Silas Gobel	Dr
To 1 mockason awl 25/100	$0.25

Siskadee November 5th	1826
Daniel Ferguson	Dr
To 1 mockason awl 25/100	$0.25

James Read	Dr
To 1 mockason awl 25/100	$0.25

Silas Gobel	Dr
To 2 yds Red Ribban	
@ 100 cts/yd	$2.00

7th

J. S. Smith	Dr
To 1 3 pt Blankett	$15.00
To 2 Skeins silk	1.00

Siskadee Octr 9th	1826 [2]
Abraham Laplant	Dr
To ½ lb Tobacco	$0.75

Arthur Black	Dr
To ½ lb Tobacco 75	$0.75

John Wilson	Dr
To 1 lb Tobacco	$1.50

John Gaiter	Dr
To 1 lb Tobacco	$1.50

John Hannah	Dr
To ½ lb Tobacco	$0.75

Daniel Ferguson	Dr
To 1 lb Tobacco	$1.50

Manuel Lazarus	Dr
To 1 lb Tobacco	$1.50

James Read	Dr
To 1 lb Tobacco	$1.50

Silas Gobel	Dr
To ½ lb Tobacco	$0.75

H. G. Rogers	Dr
To 1 lb Tobacco	$1.50

J. S. Smith	Dr
To 2 durk knives	

Ravine Encampt. Oct. 13 [3]	
Martin McCoy	Dr
To 1 Tin pan 200 cts	$2.00

Abraham Laplant	Dr
To 1 Tin pan 200 cts	$2.00

Rock Creek Encampment
November 25th

Arthur Black	Dr
To 1 Butcher Knife 100 cts	$1.00

James Reed	Cr
By 1 Pair Mockasons	
33/100	$0.33

John Gaiter	Cr
By 1 Pair Mockasons	
40/100	$0.40

J. S. Smith	Dr
To 1 Black silk Handk.	

[2] Should be Nov. 9th.

[3] Should be Nov. 13th.

Saint Gabriel   Decr 1st   1826

Arthur Black   Dr
To 1 lb Tobacco   150 cts $1.50

Saint Gabriel
December 1st   1826

Harrison G. Rogers   Dr
To 1 lb Tobacco   150 cts $1.50

Decr 5th

Robert Evans   Dr
To 1 doz Finger Rings
200 cts $2.00

Arthur Black   Dr
To ½ dozen Finger Rings
100 cts $1.00

St Gabriel   December 5th

James Reed   Dr
To ½ doz Finger Rings
100 cts $1.00

John Wilson   Dr
To ½ dozen Finger Rings
100 cts $1.00

John Hannah   Dr
To ½ doz. Finger Rings
100 cts $1.00

John Gaiter   Dr
To ½ doz. Finger Rings
100 cts $1.00

Silas Gobel   Dr
To ½ doz Finger Rings
100 cts $1.00

Abraham Laplant   Dr
To ½ dozen Finger Rings
100 cts $1.00

Martin McCoy   Dr
To ½ dozen Finger Rings
100 cts $1.00

John Wilson   Dr
To Beads   100 cts —— $1.00

Saint Gabriel
December 6th   1826

Silas Gobel   Dr
To upper Leather
150 cents $1.50

Jedediah S. Smith   Dr
1 Black Silk Handk. ——

7th

Manuel Lazarus   Dr
To ½ doz Finger Rings
100 cts $1.00

Daniel Fugerson   Dr
To ½ doz. Finger Rings
100 cts $1.00

8th

Silas Gobel   Dr
To ½ lb chewing Tobacco $0.75

John Hannah	Dr
To 1 lb chewing Tobacco	$1.50

John Gaiter	Dr
To 1 lb chewing Tobacco	$1.50

John Wilson	Dr
To 1 lb chewing Tobacco	$1.50

Abraham Laplant	Dr
To 1 lb chewing Tobacco	$1.50

James Reed	Dr
To 1 lb chewing Tobacco	$1.50

Daniel Fugerson	Dr
To 1 lb chewing Tobacco	$1.50

San Gabriel Decr 31st	1826
Arthur Black	Dr
To 1 Butcher Knife	
150 cts	$1.50

San Gabriel Jany. 4th	1827
Harrison G. Rogers	Dr
To 24 large Beads }	
To 1 Brass Ring }	

Silas Gobel	Dr
To 1 lb Tobacco	$1.50

Abraham Laplant	Dr
To 1 lb Tobacco	$1.50
To 1 Handkerchief	1.00

James Reed	Dr
To 1 lb Tobacco	$1.50
To 1 Handkerchief	1.00

[On the third-to-last page of the first section of the daybook are the following entries which refer to some personal accounts of Rogers.]

August 8th 1826 [4]		
Stanton Fitzgerald	Dr	
To H. G. Rogers	150 cts	$1.50
Sumwell Leland	Dr	
To H. G. Rogers by note		15.00
Robert Nutt	Dr	
To H. G. Rogers	75 cts	0.75

[4] This entry most likely was made at the time the Jackson-Sublette party separated from Smith's group. Of the men listed, the following disposition may be made: John Gaiter and James Read [Reed] went with Smith on the

Ephriam Logan	Dr		
To H. G. Rogers by note			4.00
James Read	Dr		
To H. G. Rogers			2.00
Jacob O'Harron	Dr		
To H. G. Rogers		75 cts	0.75
John Gaiter	Dr		
To H. G. Rogers		75 cts	$0.75
			$24.75

Arthur Black

    To H. G. Rogers   Dr

September 13th   To 2 Antelope Skins $3.00

Southwest Expedition; Stanton Fitzgerald has no other identity except through similar ledger accounts, and may or may not be the John S. Fitzgerald of Hugh Glass fame (Morgan, *Ashley*, 248 n.210) ; Jacob O'Harron [O'Hara] and Ephraim Logan continued with the firm of Smith, Jackson & Sublette and both are assumed to have been killed by Snake Indians early in 1828 although their exact fate is not known (Morgan, *Smith*, 295, 341, 344) ; Sumwell Leland cannot be traced further. Robert Nutt also appears in the Ashley ledgers for 1825 and he died in St. Louis in June, 1828 (Morgan, *Ashley*, 294 n.242). The last few months of his life must have been a nightmare, for in February, 1828, a St. Louis lawyer noted that: ". . . Nutt's mind was so deranged that he would some time suppose he was in the City of Albany where his Brother lives & sometimes on the Rocky Mountains, & when questioned about seafaring matters, he would suppose himself a Lieutenant on board his Britanic Majesty's ship . . . being asked where he was he would say sometimes in this or that place – frequently speak of the Rocky Mountains with any who might indulge a talk about Beaver Taking etc. etc. . . ." (Jan. 28, 1828, Hamilton R. Gamble Papers, MHS.)

The Narrative

[. . .] Broad, handsomely striped, the Cattle differ from ours, they have larger Horns, long legs, and thin Bodies – the Beef similar to ours, the face of the country changes hourly, Handsome Bottoms covered with grass similar to our Bluegrass the mou. grow lower, and clear of Rock to what they have been heretofore –

27th [November] we got ready as early as possible and started on a W. course, and travelled 14 m, and enc. for the day, we passed innumerable herds of cattle Horses and some hundred, of sheep we passed 4 or 5 Ind. loges that there Inds acts as Herdsmen, there come and old Ind. to us that speaks good spanish, and took us with him to his mansion, which consisted of 2 Rows of large and lengthy Buildings, after the spanish mode, they remind me of the British Barracks – so soon as we enc. there was plenty prepared to eat, a fine young cow killed, and a plenty of corn meal given us. pretty soon after the 2 commandants of the missionary establishment, come to us and had the appearance of Gentlemen

Mr S. went with them to the mansion and I stay with the company, there was great feasting among the men as they were pretty hungry not haveing any good meat for some time –

28th   Mr. S. wrote me a note in the morning stateing that he was recived as a Gentleman and treated as such, and that he wished me to go back and look for a Pistol that was lost and send the company on to the missionary establishment, I complyed with his request went Back, and found the Pistol, and arrived late in the Evening was recived very politely and showed into a room and my arms taken from me   about 10 O.Clock at night supper was served and Mr. S. and myself sent for   I was introduced to the 2 Priests over a glass of good old whisky – and found them to be Joval friendly Gentlemen the supper consisted of a number of different dishes served different from any Table I ever was at. Plenty of good wine during supper, before the cloth was removed sugar was introduced, Mr. S. has wrote to the Govenor and I expect we shall remain here some days –

29th   still at the mansion   we was sent for about sun rise to drink Tea, and eat some Bread and cheese, they all appear friendly and treat us well although they are Catholicks by profession, they allow us the liberty of conscience, and treat us as they do there own countrymen, or breatheren, about 11 O.Clock Dinner was ready and the Priest come after us to go an dine, we were invited into the office, and invited to take a glass of gin and water and eat some bread and cheese, directly after we were seated at dinner and every thing went on in style, both the Priests being pretty merry the clerk and an other Gentleman who speaks some English they all appear to be Gentlemen of the first class; both in manner and habbits – the mansion or mission consist of 4 Rows of houses forming a compleate square, where there is all kinds of macanicks at work, the Church faces the East and the guard house the west the N. and S. line comprises the work-shop, they have large vine yards, Apple and peach orchards a – some orrange Trees and some fig trees they manufacture Blankets, and sundry other articles, they distill whiskey and grind there own grain, having a water mill of tolerable quality, they have upwards of 1000 persons employed men women and children Inds of different nations – The situation is very handsome, pretty streams of water runing through from all quarters, some thousands of acres of Rich and fertile land as level as a die, in view and a part under cultivation, surrounded on the N. with high and lofty mou, handsomely timbered with pine, and ceder, and on the S. with low mou. covered with grass Cattle. this mission has upwards 30,000 head of cattle, and Horses sheep Hogs &c in proportion, I intend visiting the iner apartments to-morrow if life is spared. I am quit unwell to-day but have been engaged in writing letters for the men and drawing a map of my travels for the Priest's Mr. Smith as well as myself have been engaged in the same business – they slaughter at this place from 2 to 3000 head of cattle, at a time, the mission lives on the profits, St Gabriel is in North Latitude 34 degrees and 30 minutes it still continues warm the thermometer stands at 65 and 70 degrees –

30th Still at Saint Gabriel every thing goes on well, only the men is on a scanty allowance, as yet. there was a wedding in this place to-day, and Mr. S. and myself invited, the bell was rang a little before sun Rise, and the morning Service performed, then the musick commenced serranading the soldiers fireing &c. about 7 OClock Tea and Bread served, and about 11 Dinner and musick, the ceremony and dinner was held at the Priests, they had a elegant dinner, consisting of a number of dishes, Boiled and Roast meat and fowl, wine and Brandy or ogadent, Grapes brought as a desert after Dinner Mr. S. and myself acted quit Independent, Knot understanding there Language, nor they ours, we endeavoured to appologise, being very dirty and not in a situation to shift our colothing – but no excuse wou'd be taken, we must be present, as we have been seated at there Table ever since we arrived at this place, they treat as Gentlemen in every sense of the word, although our apparal is so indifferent, and we not being in circumstances at this time to help ourselves Being about 800 m. on a direct line from the place of our deposit, Mr. S. spoke to the commandant this evening respecting the Rations of his men, they were immediately removed into another apartment, and furnished with cooking utensils and plenty of Provision, they say for 3 or 4 days, our 2 Ind guides were imprisoned in the guard house the 2nd day after we arrived at the missionary establishment and remain confined as yet   Mr. S. wrote to the commandant of the Province, and we do not know the result as yet, or where we shall go from this place But I expect to the N.W. I intended visiting the iner apartments to-day. But have been engaged in assisting Mr. S. in making a map for the Priest, and attending the ceremonies of the wedding –

December 1st 1826 – we still remain at the mansion of St Gabriel things going on as usual, all friendship and peace, Mr. S. let his Blacksmiths James Reed and Silas Gobel to work in the B.S. Shop to make a Bare Trap for the Priest, agreeable to promise yesterday, Mr. S. and the Interpreter went in the evening to the next mission which is 9 m distance from St Gab. and called St Pedro, A spanish Gentleman from that mission having sent his servant with horses for him, there came an Italian Gentleman, from Port Sandiego to day by the name of John Battis, Bonafast [5] who speaks good English, and acts as Interpreter for all the American and English vessels that arrives in Port on the coast, quite a smart and inteligent man, The men all appear satisfied since there was new regulations made about eating, Mr. S. informed me this morning that he had to give read a little floggin yesterday evening, on account of

[5] Juan B. Bonifacio.

some of his impertinence, he appeared more complisant to-day than usual, Our fare at Table much the same as at first, a plenty of every thing good to eat and drink.

2nd much the same to-day as yesterday, both being what the Catholicks call fast days, in the morning, after sun Rise, or about that time, you have Tea Bread and cheese at dinner fish and fowl, Beans, Peas, Potatoes and other kinds of sauce, Grapes as a desert, wine Gin and water plenty at dinner – I cou'd see a great deal of satisfaction here if I cou'd talk there Language – But as it is I feel great diffidence in being among them Knot Knowing the Topic of there conversation still every attention is paid to me by all that is present, especially the old Priest, I must say he is a very fine man, and a very much of a Gentleman. Mr. S. has not returned from the other mission as yet. The Province is called the Province of New Callifornia, This mission ships to Europe annually from 20 to 25 thousand dollars worth of skins and Tallow and about 20 thousand dollars worth of soap. There vineyards are extensive, they make there own wine, and Brandy the have orranges and Limes, growing here, The Inds appear to be much alltered from the wild indians in the mou, that we have passed they are kept in great fear, for the least offence they are corrected, they are compleat slaves in every sense of the word —— Mr. S. and Laplant returned late in the evening, and represents, their treatment to be good at the other mission. Mr. S. tells me that Mr.

Francisco [6] the spanish Gentleman that he went to visit promises him, as many Horses and mules as he wants, –

December 3rd   Sunday   About 6 O.Clock the Bell rang for mass, and they poured into church from all quarters, men, women and children, there was none of us invited therefore we all remained at our own lodgings – The fare to day at Table much as usual there was an additional cup of Tea in the afternoon. The Inds play bandy with sticks, it being the only Game I have seen as yet among them, they play before the Priests door, I am told they dance with spanyards and Inds. in the course of the Evening –

4th   still at St Gabriel, things much as usual, The Priest presented Mr. S. with 2 pieces of shirting containing 64 yards, for to make the men shirts, all being nearly naked. Mr. Smith gave each man 3½ yards and kept the same number for himself. Each man getting enough to make a shirt, the weather still continues to be moderate, the Thermometer stands at 60 and 63 in the days, & 50-53 in the night, the Thermometer hangs within doors – &c

5th   we are still remaining at the mansion of St Gabriel, waiting the result of the governor's answer, to a letter that Mr. S. addressed to him on the 27th of November   we expect the courier some time to day with letters. it still continues moderate –

---

[6] Francisco Avila.

6th   Early this morning I presented the old priest with my Buffalo robe, and he Brought me a very large Blanket and presented me, in return about 10 O.Clock, (nothing new) things going on as they have been heretofore, no answer from the Governor as yet, – we are waiting with patience, to hear from the Govenor, –

7th   No answer as yet from the Govenor of the Province, Mr. S. and all hands getting impatient, There was a Spanish Gentleman arrived yesterday named Francis Martinnis [7] a very intelligent man, who speaks pretty good English, and appears very friendly, he advises Mr. S. to go see the Govenor in case he does not recieve an answer in a few days – he is a man of Business and is well aware that men on Expences, and Business of importance, should be preservering – he appears anxious as respects our wellfare – Mr. S. has some Idea of going in company with him to Sandiego – the residence of the Govenor –

8th   Nothing of importance has taken place to day. Mr. S. was sent for to go to Sandiego – to see the Govenor, Capt. Cuningham, commanding the ship Courier, now lying in port at Sandiego, arrived here late this Evening, the captain is a Bostonian and has been trading on the coast for Hides and Tallow since June last, he informs me that he is rather under the impression that he shall be obliged to remain untill some time in

---

[7] Francisco Martinez.

the succeeding summer in consequence of so much op-
position, as there is a number of vessels on the coast
trading for the same kind of articles, he says that money
is very scarce, amongst the most of People, Mr. Martina
tells me that there is Between 16 or 17,000 natives that
is converted over to the Catholic faith and under the
control of the different missions, the white Population
he estimates at 6,000 making 22 or 23,000 thousand
souls in the Province of New Callifornia

9th   Mr. Smith and one of the men in company with
Capt Cuningham left San Gabriel, this morning for
sandiego, the Govenors place of residence, I expect he
will be absent for eight or ten days. – the weather still
keeps moderate, things much the same. (friendship and
peace as yet)

10th   Sunday   There was five Inds. Brought to the
mission by two other Inds – who act as constables, or
overseers and sentenced to be whiped for not going to
work when ordered   Each recieved from 12 to 14
lashes on there Bare Posteriors   they were all old men
say from 50 to 60 years of age, the commandant standing by with his sword, to see that the Ind. who flogged
them done his duty – things in other respects similar
to the last sabbath –

11th   Nothing of consequence has Taken place to-day
more than usual, only the Band of musick consisting of
Two small violins, one Bass violin a trumpet and tri-

angle was played for 2 hours in the evening before the Priests door by Inds – they made Tolerable good music, the most in imitation to whites that ever heard, directly after the musick wou'd cease, there was several rounds of Cannon fired by the soldiers, in commemoration of some great Saints day or feast day – they kept at this place 4 small fixed pieces, 2 – 6 pounders and 2 – 2 pounders to protect them from the Inds – in case they shou'd rebel. and from the best information I can get from the soldiers they appear at times some what alarmed for fear the Inds – will rise and destroy the mission, –

12th   About sun Rise, the Bell Rang – and mass called, men women and children attended church, they discharged a number of small arms and some cannon while the morning service were performing – There main church is upwards of 200 feet in length and about 140 in Breadth made of stone and Brick, a number of different apartments in it, they hold meating in the Large Church every sunday, the spanyards first attend and then the Inds – they have a room, in the iner apartment of the mission to hold church on there feast days – There Religion appears to be a form more than a reality – I am in hopes we shall be able to leave here in five or six days at most, as all hands appear to be anxious to move on to the north, things in other respects much the same, the weather still continues to be good – In the Evening there was a kind of procession amongst Both

Spanyards & Inds – I enquired the reason, I was told by a Mr. David Philips[8] an Englishman that this day a year ago the Virgin Mary appeared to an Ind. and told him that the 12th day of December shou'd always be Kept as a feast day and likewise a Holliday among them and both the spanyards and Inds believe it –

13th   I walked through the work shops, I saw some Inds – Blacksmithing some, carpentering, others making the wood work of ploughs, others employed in making spining wheels for the squaws, to spin on there is upward 60 women employed in spining yarn and others weaving, things much the same, cloudy and some Rain to-day, our Black Smith have been employed for several days making horse Shoes and nails, for our own use, when we leave here –

14th   I was asked by the Priest to let our Blacksmith, make a large trap for him to set in his orrange Garden to catch Inds Inn, when they come up at night to rob his orchard – The weather clear and warm, things in other respects much as they have been heretofore, friendship and peace prevail with us and the spanyards – our own men are contintious and quarrelsome amongst themselves and have been ever since we started the Expedition   last night at supper for the first time the Priest questioned me as respected my religion. I very

8 David Philips is possibly the English cooper who is recorded first in San Diego in 1834 (Bancroft, *History of California*, IV, 776) as identified in Dale, 205 n.422.

frankly informed him that I was brought up under the Calvanist doctrine, and did not believe that it was in the power of man to forgive sins. God only had that power – and when I was under the necessity of confessing my sins, I confided them unto God in pray, and supplication not to man, I further informed him that it was my opinion that man ought to possess, as well as profess Religion to constitute the Christian – he said that when he was in his church and his robe on he then believed that he was equal unto God, and had the power to forgive any sin, that man were guilty of and openly confessed unto him, but when he was out of church and his common waring apparel on he was as other men, divested of all power of forgiveing sins –

15th I went out fowling with the commandant of the mission, I killed 7 Brant and one Duck, and the commandant killed 2 Brant and one Duck, the priest furnished me with shot, Two of our men went to work to-day Arthur Black and John Gaiter, they are to get a horse a piece for 3 days work, times much the same as they have been some time back, nothing new occurs.

16th late this evening a Mr Henry [9] owner of a Brig now lying in port, arrived at the Mission, he appears to be a very much of a Gentleman, and quit intelligent his Business her is to buy hides, Tallow and soap, from

9 Given later as Henry Edwards (*see* entry for Dec. 18), the man may well be Henry Adams, who was master of the Hamburg-based schooner *Paraiso* (or *Paradise*) which was consigned to Mancisidor in 1827 (Bancroft, *History of California*, III, 148). Possibly Rogers misunderstood the name.

the priest, nothing new has taken place. – Things much the same about the mission, the Priest adminerated the sacrament to a sick Indian to-day, that he thinks will die.

Two days above Saint Francisco, plenty Beaver at a Lake   Three days above Santa Clare, River Pireadaro, Two Laries or Flag Lakes Plenty of Beaver, as we are informed by Mr Martinos, ——[10]

17th   The sick Indian, that the Priest adminerated the sacrament to yesterday died last night and was entered in there grave yard this evening the proceedings in Church similar to the last sabbath – sunday appears to be the day that the most Business is transacted at this mission the Priest Plays at cards both Sunday and weak a days, when he has company that can play pretty expert ——

18th   I received a Letter from Mr. S. informing me, that he rather was under the impression, that he wou'd be detained, for some time yet, as the Govenor did not

---

[10] This note appears twice in the daybook in slightly different locations and versions at about this point in the text. Of the places mentioned, San Francisco refers to the San Francisquito Creek and Canyon area in the mountains just north of San Gabriel, a well-traveled Indian trail leading into Antelope Valley and ultimately on to the lakes in the San Joaquin Valley. Santa Clare is the Santa Clara River, and the River Pireadaro (or Piradara, as it is also spelled), is probably Rogers' version of *La Porciuncula,* the name given by Fr. Zalvidea in 1806 to what is now the Kern River. The lakes, of course, are a reference to the Lake Tulare, Lake Buena Vista, and Kern Lake area of the southern San Joaquin Valley.

like to take the responsibility on himself to let us pass untill he received instructions from the General, in Mexico, under those circumstances I am fearful we still have to remain here some time yet, our men have been employed putting out a cargo of hides, Tallow and soap for a Mr Henry Edwards, a German by birth, and the most intelligent man that I have met with since I arrived at this place – he is what they term here a mexican Trader ――――

Mr. S. also wrote to me for Eight Beaver skins to present to the spanish officers to face there cloaks with, I complied with his request and selected eight of the Best and sent to him,

19th   Still remaining at San Gabriel things much the same, I went out with my Gun, to amuse myself, killed some Black Birds and Ducks   The express left here this morning for sandiego, I sent the eight Beaver skins, to Mr. Smith to present to the spanish officers to face there cloaks, by him   the old Father, continues his friendship to me it does not appear to abate in the least. I still eat at his Table, this mission if properly managed wou'd be equal to mines, of silver, or gold. there farms is extensive, they raise from 3 to 4000 Bushels of wheat annually and sell to the shippers for 3,00 pr Bushel, there annual income situated as it is and managed so badly by the Inds. is worth in hides Tallow soap wine, ogadent, wheat and corn from 55 to 60,000 dollars ――――

20th   Nothing new has taken place, all peace and

friendship. I expect an answer from Mr Smith in six or eight days if he does not get permission to pass on, my situation is a very delicate one, as I have to by amongst the grandees of the country ever day . . . more or less and have no clothes to shift myself all the clothing I have consisting of a leather hunting shirt, Blankett Pantaloons two shirts, pr of sock, shoes and read cap —— I make a very Grotesques appearance when seated at Table amongst the dandys with there ruffles silks and Broadcloths, and I am

[End of the first segment]

A NEW YEARS ADDRESS, BY HARRISON G. ROGERS
TO THE REVEREND FATHER OF SAN GABRIEL MISSION,
JANUARY 1st 1827 ———

Reverend Father,

Standing on the threshold of a new year, I salute you with the most cordial congratulations and good wishes.

While the sustaining providence of God has given us a nother year of probation, every thing seems to remind me, that is for probation.

Many, very many, during the past year, have, doubtless, been called throughout the different parts of the trackless Globe to weep over friends now sleeping in their graves – many others have personally felt the visitation of sickness – and probably many more, ere another year, ushers in, will be called from time into eternity.

While revolving seasons – while sickness disappointment and death raise their minatory voice, remember, Reverend Sir, that this world is not our home; – It is a world of trial – It is the dawn of an immortal existence.

Therefore my advise, is, to all the human family, to be faithful, be devoted to God; be kind; be benevolent to their fellow sufferers: – to act well their part: – live for eternity; for the everlasting destinies of their souls is suspended upon their probation, and this may close the present year.

Our saviour Sir, after having spent his life in untrying benevolence, and before he ascended to his native heavens, probably in allusion to the twelve tribes of Isreal; elected twelve apostles or missionaries.

To these after having properly qualified and instructed them, he left a part of his legacy, a world to be converted.

He directed that "repentance and remission of sins, should be preached, in his name among all nations, beginning at Jerusalem." Agreeably to his command the first church was founded at Jerusalem.

But Reverend Father, remember the whole world was missionary ground. Before the day of Christ, Jesus our Saviour we never heard of missionaries to the Heathens – with a solitary exception.

The exception to which I allude is the case of Jonah, who was sent to preach to the heathen at Ninevah, about 800 years before Christ.

It was not till several years after the ascension of our saviour that a Single Gentile was converted. The Apostles hesitated – delayed no longer. It is said by ancient history, that the world was divided among them by lot.

Be this as it may, it is certain that they soon separated, and went from village to village.

To this little number of missionaries we are informed that Paul was soon added.

With the exception of this man, the missionaries were not learned in the arts and sciences; were ignorant of books and of men: yet they went forth unsupported by human aid – friendless – opposed by prejudices, laws, learning, reasonings of Philosophy, passions and persecutions.

And what was the result of their labours? We know but a little; we can trace only a few of their footsteps. Yet we know enough to astonish us. We know that by the labour of those missionaries there are mentioned in the New Testament sixty-seven different places in which christian churches were established by them – some of which places, contained several churches.

Paul informs us that in his time the Gospel had been preached to every [nation] which is under heaven. Justin Martyr tells us that in the year 106, "There was not a nation, either Greek or Barbarian, or of any other name even of those who wander in tribes and live in tents, among whom prayers and thanksgiving are not offered to the Father and Creator of the Universe, by the name of the Crucified Jesus." we know assuredly that at this time, that there were Churches in Germany, Spain, France and Brittain. Besides the apostles, there were at least sixty-seven Evangelists in this age, so that the whole number of active missionaries in the Apostolic age, was ninety-nine or, one hundred. Of the apostles, we have reasons to believe, nine, at least. suffered martyrdom. On the whole, then, we have no reason to doubt, on the Testamony, of history and tradition, that the last command of Christ was so obeyed, that in the Apostolic age, the Gospel was preached in every part of the Globe which was then known.

Monday January 1st 1827 This morning Church, was held before day men, women and children attended as usual, after church musick played by the Ind.s, as on Sunday, wine and some other articles of clothing given out to the inds – the Priest keeps a memorandum of all articles issued to them, the fare at Table the same as other days, if any difference not so good, some Rain last night, and to-day. weather warm, showers alternate through the day like may showers in the states, and equally as pleasant, things in other respects much the same. no news from Mr. S. and I am at a loss how to act in his absence, with the company as he left no special instructions with me when he left here.

Tuesday 2nd   still at the mission of San Gabriel, nothing new has taken place to-day. the men commenced work again this morning for the old Padra, no news from Mr. S. friendship and peace still prevail. Mr. Joseph Chapman, a Bostonian by Birth, who is married in this country and brought over to the catholic faith, came here about 10 OClock A.M. to superintend the burning of a coal pit, for the Priest, he is getting wealthy, being what we term a yanky, he is jack of all trades, and naturally a very inginious man, under the circumstances he gets many favours from, the Priest, by superintending the building of mills, Blacksmithing, and many other Branches of machanism –

W. 3rd   There was five, or six Inds. brought to the mission and whiped, and one of them, being stubborn, and did not like to submit to the lash was knocked down, by the commandant, tied and severly shiped, then chained by the leg to another Ind. who had been guilty of a similar offence. I recvd a letter from Mr. S. this morning informing me, that he had got his passport signed by the Govenor, by the intercession of the Gentlemen officers, and that he would join me in a few days – he intended embarking on Board Capt Cuninghams ship, and coming to St. Pedro which is forty five miles distance from San Gabriel.

Thurs 4th   Still at the mission, nothing new, four of our men, Robert Evans, Manuel Lazarus, John Hannah and John Wilson, went with Mr Joseph Chapman, to cut wood for the coal pile, and assist him in erecting it, and Burning the coal, myself and Mr. McCoy went up the mountains, to see if we could find some Bear. I saw two and wounded one, killed a wolf and two Ducks. Mr. McCoy saw two Dear, and got one shot but missed, we passed through a great abundance of oak Timber, some trees heavy loaden with acorns, the land rich and easy cultivated   Some large springs or Lagoons which afford a great quantity of water, which is brought, in all directions through the mission farm, as they have to water there orchards gardens and farms ——

Friday 5th   Still remaining at the mission San Gabriel, waiting the arrival of Mr. S. five men went with Mr Chapman this morning to cut cord wood for the coal pile   I walked over the soap factory and find it more extensive, than I had an Idea, it consists of 4 large cisterns, as Boilers that will hold from 2000 to 25000 hundred gallons each the cistern is built in the shape of a sugar loaf, made of Brick, stone and lime, there is a large iron Pott, or Kettle, fixed in the bottom, where the fire strikes them to set them Boiling, lined a round the mouth of the cistern, and edge of the potts with sheet Iron 8 or 10 inches wide, the potts or kettles will hold from 2 to 250 gallons each – and a great many smaller ones, fixed in like manner, things in other respects much the same about the mission as usual, friendship and peace with us and the spanyards –

6th   Saturday   this being what is called Epihany or old Christmas day it is kept to celebrate the manifestation of Christ to the Gentiles, or particularly the maji, or wise men from the East, church held early as usual,

men, women and children attend, after church the ceremonies as on Sundays wine issued abundantly to both
Spanyards and Inds – musick played by the Ind. Band
– after the issue of the morning, our men in company
with some spayards – went and fired a salute, the old
Padra give them wine, Bread & meat as a treat. – Some
of the men got drunk and two of them James Reed and
Daniel Fugerson commenced fighting, and some of the
spayards interfered, and struck one of our men by the
name of Black, which came very near in terminating
with bad consequences – as soon, as I heard of the dis-
turbance, I went among them, and pacified our men, by
telling what trouble they were bringing upon themselves in case they did not desist and the most of them
being men of reason adheared to my advice – our Blacksmith James Reed, came very abruptly into the Priests
dining room while at dinner, and asked for orgadent,
the Priest ordered a plate of victuals to be handed to
him, he eat a few mouthfulls, and set the Plate on the
Table, and then took up the Decanter of wine, and
drunk without any invitation, and came very near Braking the glass when he set it down. the Padra seeing he
was in a state of inebriety, refrained from saying any
thing –

Sunday 7th   Things arried on, as on former sabaths
since I have been at the mission, church Services, morning, and evening, issues to the Inds of wine & clothing.
The Priest in the evening threw orranges among the

young squaws to see them scuffle, the activiest and strongest would get the greatest share, Mr. S. has not joined us at yet

Monday 8th last night there was a great Fandango, or dance among the spanyards – they kept it up till nearly day light from the noise, the women here are very unchaste, all that I have seen, and heard speak appear very vulgar in their conversations, and manners – they think it an honnour to ask a white man to sleep with them, one came to my lodgings last night and asked me to make here a Blanco Pickaninia, which being interpreted, is to get here a white child – and I must say for the first time I was a shamed, and did not gratify her, or comply with here request seeing here so forward I had no propencity to tech here – things about the mission much the same. No news of Mr. S. and I am very impatient, waiting his arrival –

9th Tuesday Business going on about the mission as usual, about 8 or 10 Boys employed gathering orranges overseed by the commandant and steward of the mission old Antonia, a man of 65 years of age, who is entrusted with the Keys, of all the stores belonging to the mission he generally is served at the Priests Table, and from appearance is very saving and trusty. I went out in company with Mr. McCoy this evening with our guns, to amuse ourselves. I killed One Brant, and Mr. McCoy killed nothing. Mr. S. still absent from the company.

Wednesday 10th About noon Mr. S. Capt. Cuningham, Mr. Shaw, and Thos Dodges[11] came to the mission from the ship Courier and I was much rejoiced to see them as I have been waiting with anxiety to see him, nothing new has taken place to-day, things much the same, about the Mission – Mr. S. intends going Back in the morning to the ship

Thursday 11th   Mr. S. in company with Capt. Cuningham, Mr. Shaw and Chapman, left the Mission this morning for the sea shore, about noon Capt Cuningham return to the mission, and informed me that Mr. S. wished me to go to the Parbalo, to buy horses wich is 8 miles distance from San Gabriel – I complyed with his request went, and met Mr. S. there, and purchased two horses for our trap, and Mr. S. made and agreement for 14 more for which he is to give merchandize at the ship in exchange

Friday 12th   I got the two horses we Bought last evening from Mr. Francis Abbelo,[12] and returned to the mission about the middle of the day. just as I arrived the Priest from San whan[13] arrived on a visit, with his carriage, and Indian servants, he is a man about 50 years of age upwards, of six feet high, and well made in proportion, and from his conduct he appears to be a very good man, and a much of a gentleman   I had, a Branding Iron, made by our Blacksmith so soon as I re-

---

[11] Thomas Dodge of the *Courier* is not mentioned in Smith's narrative.

[12] Francisco Avila, again.

[13] The priest from San Juan Capistrano is Fr. José Barona (1764-1831) who served at the mission from 1811 until his death.

turned, and Branded the two horses that we Bought, with J.S. things in other respects about the mission much the same.

Saturday, 13th   This morning I set the men to work, to put the traps in order for packing, one of the horses I brought yesterday got loose last night and ran off, and I have not got him yet or heard anything of him, to-day at dinner I was asked a great many questions By the Priest who came here yesterday, respecting our rout and travels, I give him all the satisfaction I cou'd, and informed him as respects the situation of the country I have traveled through, also the United States, and their laws, things about the mission much as usual ——

Sunday 14th   As agreeable to promise I sent Arthur Black, John Gaiter and Peter Ranne to the Parbalo, to meet Mr. Smith to get horses, which he is purchasing at that place – time is passing off swiftly and we are not under way yet, But I am in hopes we shall be able to start in three or 4 days from here – Church, as usual, wine issued &c. In the evening four Inds who had been fighting and gambleing was brought before the guard House Door, and sentenced to be whiped   they recived from 30 to 40 lashes each on their Bare Posteriors –

Monday 15th   About noon Capt. Cuningham and Mr. Chapman arrived at the mission from the ship. Mr. S. still remain in the Parbalo, purchasing Horses, Mr. Chapman informed me that there is a natural pitch river north of the Parbalo 8 or 10 miles where there is from 40 to 50 hogsheads, of pitch throwed up from the Bowels of the Earth, daily, The Citizens of the Country make great use of it to pitch the roofs of there Houses – he shew me a piece which have the smell of stone coal, mor than any other thing I can describe, Business about the mission much the same, as it has been heretofore, I went in there church to-day for the first time – and saw there molten Images, they have our Saviour on the cross, his mother and Mary the mother of James, and 4 of the apostles, all as large as life, They appropriate the room, where the Images stand, to a sugar Factory –

Tuesday 16th   Mr. S. returned from the Parbelo, with 41 head of horses which he purchased at that place, he got 8 new saddles from the Padra, and set the men to work, – to fix them, nothing new has taken place about the mission, things much the same.

Wednesday 17th   All hands are Busily employed, fixing there things ready to start to-morrow morning. The Old Father has given a great deal to Mr. Smith, and some of the men, and continues givin I expect we shall be able to get off early in the morning, – things about the mission much the same

Thursday 18th   All hands were up early this morning, and went to the pen, where we had our horses 48 in number, and got them packed, and under way in pretty good season, after we got ½ mile off the mission, our unpacked Horses, together with them that had packs on started to run 8 or 10 miles Before we stoped them, one of the pack Horses, lossed 12 dressed skins, that Mr. S. had got, from our old Father, of San gabriel Mission Joseph Sannes, we travelled a direct course N.S. about 4 m. and we at an Ind. farm House where we, stayed on the 27th November, when we first reached the spanish Inhabitants, Mr. S. and myself intend returning to the mission, this evening ——

Friday 19th   Mr. S. and myself returned to the mission, late last evening and took supper, with Old father Sancus, for the last time, and our Farewell. the old Father give each of us a Blankett, and give me a cheese, and a gourd filled with ogadent. All hands being ready early in the morning, we started and travelled, and had an Ind. guide a N.E. course about, 25 m, and enc – at St. Ann, and Ind. farm House, for the night, our wild horses created us considerable, trouble during the day.

Saturday 20th   Still at St. Ann, Mr. S. comands to lie by to-day, as there is five of our best horses missing, and hunt them, and Brake some other Horses, a number of the men are employed hunting Horses and others haltering and Brake, more, The horse hunters returned with out finding them, and he intends leaving them, and proceeding on his journey early to morrow morning.

Sunday 21st   All hands were up early and getting there horses packed, we were under way in pretty good season, in the morning, and had an Ind Boy as a pilot, we started and travelled a N.E. and By East course 25 or

30 m. and reached and Ind. farm house, about 4 m. distant from San Bern,a,do and enc – where we have and order, from the govenor, and, our old Father Joseph Sanchus at the mission of San Gabriel, for all the supplys we stand in need of – the country quit mountainous and stoney –

Monday 22nd   Mr. S. and the Interpreter started early this morning up to San Bernandano for to see the Steward, and get surplys we intend killing some Beef here and drying meat. I expect we shall remain here two or three days – all hands get milk this morning —— we have killed two Bulls and cut the meat, and drying it. Mr. S. has got corn, peas, parched meal, and flour of wheat, old Father Sanchius has been the greatest friend that I ever meet with, with all my Travels, he is worthy of being called a christian as he possesses charity in the highest degree – and a friend to the poor and distressed, I ever shall hold him as man of God, taking us when in distress feeding and clothing us – and may god prosper him and all such men, when we left the mission he give Mr. S. and order to get every thing he wanted for the use of his company, at San Burnandeino – the steward complyed with the order so soon as it was presented by Mr. S.

Tuesday 23rd   Still at the Ind. farm 3 m from San-burnandeino, some of the men are employed in braking Horses, and others makeing pack saddles and riggin them, Mr. S. sent a letter back this morning to Old

Father Sanchius concerning the Horses we lossed at Saint Ann, six in number, he will wait the result of his answer

Wednesday 24th   We are still remaining at the Ind. farm, waiting the result of the Priests answer, and drying meat, and repairing saddles for our journey. some of the men are kept employed braking wild Horses, Daniel Ferguson one of our men, when leaving the mission on the 18th Inst. Hide himself and we could not find him. the corporal who commands at the mission promised to find him, and send him on to us. But I expect we shall not see him again. the weather continues fine,

Thursday 25th   No answer from the Priest this morning, and we are obliged to remain here another day. The man still kept at work, braking young Horses. Mr. S. discharged one of the men John Wilson, on the 17th Inst. and he cou'd not get permission to stay in the country. therefore we obliged to let him come back to us. he remains with the company but not under pay as yet. I expect he will go on with us ——— The weather still continues Beautiful – things about our camp much as usual   Inds – travelling, back and forward from the mission steady – the Inds here call themselves the Farrahoots.

Friday 26th   Early this morning we collected our Horses – and counted them and two was missing. Mr. S. sent a man in search of them, he returned with them about 10 OClock, we are still at the Ind – farm House, waiting an answer from the Priest – at San Gabriel. I expect we shall remain here to-day – if the courier does not arrive, in the evening James Reed and myself concluded we would go into the cowpen and rope some cows, and milk them, after the Ind – fashion, accordingly we made ready, our rope, and haltered four cows, and tied there heads up to a steak, and made fast there hind feet and milked them, But did not get much milk on account of not letting there calves to them. so soon as we were done Capt Smith and Silas Gobel followed our example, this country in many respects is the most desireable part of the world I ever was in, the climate so regular and Beautiful, the Thermometer, stands daily from 65 to 70 degrees – and I am told it is about the same in summer ——

Saturday 27th   Mr. S. swaped six of our old horses off for wild mares, – Still at the Ind. farm House waiting the answer from the priest, 20 of our horses missing this morning – and four men sent in search of them. Mr. S. and Laplant, is gone up to San Burnandeino to see the old steward on Business –

[End of the second segment]

Bibliography
and
Index

Bibliography

MANUSCRIPTS

William H. Ashley Papers, Missouri Hist. Soc., St. Louis
Robert Campbell Papers, Missouri Hist. Soc., St. Louis
Hamilton R. Gamble Papers, Missouri Hist. Soc., St. Louis
Pettus Collection, Missouri Hist. Soc., St. Louis
Jedediah S. Smith Manuscript, The Jennewein Western Coll., Dakota
    Wesleyan Univ., Mitchell, S.D.
Jedediah S. Smith Papers, Missouri Hist. Soc., St. Louis
William L. Sublette Papers, Missouri Hist. Soc., St. Louis

BOOKS AND PERIODICALS

ALTER, J. Cecil (ed.) *Life in the Rocky Mountains 1830-1835,* by
    Warren Angus Ferris. Salt Lake City, 1940
———— (ed.) "W. A. Ferris in Utah 1830-1835," *Utah Hist. Qtly.,*
    IX, 1-2 (Jan.-Apr., 1941), 81-108
"AN AMERICAN" [Alfred Robinson]. *Life in California, During a
    Residence of Several Years in That Territory.* New York, 1846
BANCROFT, Hubert Howe. *California Pioneer Register and Index,
    1542-1848.* Baltimore, 1964
————. *History of California.* 7 vols. San Francisco, 1884-1890

BEALE, Edward F. *Wagon Road from Fort Defiance to the Colorado River.* Wash., D.C., 1858

BEATTIE, George William, and Helen Pruitt Beattie. *Heritage of the Valley; San Bernardino's First Century.* Pasadena, 1939

BECKER, Robert H. *Thomas Christy's Road Across the Plains.* Denver, 1969

BECKWITH, E.G. "Report of Exploration for a Route for the Pacific Railroad by Capt. J. W. Gunnison, Etc. . . ," *Reports of Explorations and Surveys, to Ascertain the Most Practicable and Economical Route for a Railroad from the Mississippi River to the Pacific Ocean* . . . *1853-4.* 12 vols. in 13. Wash., D.C., 1856

BERGER, John A. *The Franciscan Missions of California.* New York, 1941

BOLTON, Herbert E. "In the South San Joaquin Ahead of Garces," *Qtly. of the Calif. Hist. Soc.,* X, no. 3 (Sept. 1931), 211-19

BONNER, T.D. *The Life and Adventures of James P. Beckwourth, Mountaineer, Scout, and Pioneer, and Chief of the Crow Nation of Indians.* New York, 1856

CARTER, Charles Franklin (tr.) "Duhaut-Cilly's Account of California in the Years 1827-8," *Qtly. of the Calif. Hist. Soc.,* VIII, no. 2 (June 1929), 130-66; no. 3 (Sept. 1929), 214-50; no. 4 (Dec. 1929), 306-56

CARTER, Harvey L. "Jedediah Smith," *The Mountain Men and the Fur Trade of the Far West,* Vol. VIII. Glendale, Calif., 1971

COUES, Elliott (ed.) *On the Trail of a Spanish Pioneer: The Diary and Itinerary of Francisco Garcés.* 2 vols. New York, 1900

CRAMPTON, C. Gregory, and Gloria G. Griffen [Cline]. "The San Buenaventura, Mythical River of the West," *Pac. Hist. Rev.,* XXV, no. 2 (May 1956), 163-71

CUNNINGHAM, William H. *"Log of the "Courier," 1826-1827-1828.* Los Angeles, 1958

DALE, Harrison C. *The Ashley-Smith Explorations and the Discovery of a Central Route to the Pacific 1822-1829.* Glendale, Calif., 1941

DANA, Richard Henry, Jr. *Two Years Before the Mast.* Boston, 1911

ELLISON, William Henry (ed.) "Recollections of Historical Events in California, By William A. Streeter," *Calif. Hist. Soc. Qtly.,* XVIII, no. 2 (June 1939), 157-79

ENGELHARDT, Zephyrin, O.F.M. *San Gabriel Mission and the Beginnings of Los Angeles.* San Gabriel, Calif., 1927

———. *San Juan Capistrano Mission.* Los Angeles, 1922

———. *San Luis Rey Mission.* San Francisco, 1921

FARQUHAR, Francis P. *History of the Sierra Nevada.* Berkeley, Calif., 1965

———. "Jedediah Smith and the First Crossing of the Sierra Nevada," *Sierra Club Bull.,* XXVIII, no. 3 (June 1943), 35-52

——— (ed.) "The Topographical Reports of Lieutenant George H. Derby," *Qtly. of the Calif. Hist. Soc.,* X, no. 2 (June 1932), 99-123; no. 3 (Sept. 1932), 247-65

FEDERAL WRITERS' PROJECT. *Utah, a Guide to the State.* New York, 1945

FRÉMONT, John Charles. *Report of the Exploring Expedition to the Rocky Mountains in the Year 1842, and to Oregon and North California in the Years 1843-'44.* Wash., D.C., Gates & Seaton, printers, 1845

GEIGER, Maynard, O.F.M. *Franciscan Missionaries in Hispanic California.* San Marino, Calif., 1969

GUDDE, Erwin G. *California Place Names.* Berkeley, Calif., 1949

HAFEN, LeRoy, and Ann W. Hafen (eds.) *Gwinn Harris Heap, "Central Route to the Pacific. With Related Material on Railroad Exploration, etc. . . 1853-1854." Far West and Rockies Series,* Vol. VII, Glendale, Calif., 1957

HAFEN, LeRoy, and Ann W. Hafen *The Old Spanish Trail: Santa Fe to Los Angeles. Far West and Rockies Series,* vol. I, Glendale, Calif., 1954

HALL, James (?). "Captain Jedediah Strong Smith. A Eulogy of That Most Romantic and Pious of Mountainmen, First American by Land into California," *Ill. Mon. Mag.,* XXII (June 1832), 393-98

IVES, Joseph C. *Report upon the Colorado River of the West, Explored in 1857 and 1858.* Wash., D.C., 1861

JACKSON, Donald, and Mary Lee Spence. *The Expeditions of John Charles Frémont.* 2 vols. Urbana, Ill., 1970, 1973

JAEGER, Edmund C. *The North American Deserts.* Stanford, Calif., 1957

KELLY, Charles. *Salt Desert Trails.* Salt Lake City, 1930

KROEBER, Alfred Louis. *Handbook of the Indians of California.* Wash., D.C., Smithsonian Institution, 1925

LEADABRAND, Russ. *A Guidebook to the Mojave Desert of California.* Los Angeles, 1966

MALONEY, Alice Bay. "The Richard Campbell Party of 1827," *Calif. Hist. Soc. Qtly.,* XVIII, no. 4 (Dec. 1939), 347-54

MERRIAM, C. Hart. "Earliest Crossings of the Deserts of Utah and Nevada to Southern California: Route of Jedediah S. Smith in 1826," *Qtly. of the Calif. Hist. Soc.,* II, no. 2 (July 1923), 228-36

———. "Jedediah Smith's Route Across the Sierra in 1827," *Qtly. of the Calif. Hist. Soc.,* III, no. 1 (Apr. 1924), 25-29

MILLER, David E. (ed.) "Peter Skene Ogden's Journal of his Expedition to Utah, 1825," *Utah Hist. Qtly.,* XX, no. 2 (Apr. 1952), 159-86

MORGAN, Dale L. *Jedediah Smith and the Opening of the West.* Indianapolis, 1953

———. *The West of William H. Ashley.* Denver, 1964

———, and Eleanor Towles Harris (eds.) *The Rocky Mountain Journals of William Marshall Anderson — The West in 1834.* San Marino, Calif., 1967

Bibliography

———, and Carl I. Wheat. *Jedediah Smith and his Maps of the American West.* San Francisco, 1954

OGDEN, Adele. "Hide and Tallows, McCulloch, Hartnell and Company, 1822-1828," *Qtly. of the Calif. Hist. Soc.,* VI, no. 3 (Sept. 1927), 254-264

PEIRSON, Erma. *The Mohave River and Its Valley.* Glendale, Calif., 1970

PETERSON, Roger Tory. *A Field Guide to Western Birds.* Boston, 1961

POURADE, Richard F. *Time of the Bells.* San Diego, 1961

ROBINSON, William W. *Los Angeles from the Days of the Pueblo.* San Francisco, 1959

ST. LOUIS, *Missouri Saturday News*

SAN DIEGO FEDERAL WRITERS' PROJECT. *San Diego, A California City.* San Diego, 1937

SITGREAVES, Lorenzo. *Report of an Expedition down the Zuni and Colorado Rivers, by Capt. L. Sitgreaves, Corps Topographical Engineers.* . . Wash., D.C., 1853

SULLIVAN, Maurice S. *Jedediah Smith, Trader and Trail Breaker.* New York, 1936

——— (ed.) *The Travels of Jedediah Smith.* Santa Ana, Calif., 1934

SUNDER, John E. *Bill Sublette: Mountain Man.* Norman, Okla., 1959

WEBER, David J. *The Taos Trappers.* Norman, Okla., 1971

WEBER, The Rev. Francis J. *Catholic Footprints in California.* Newhall, Calif., 1970

WEDEL, Waldo R. "Archeological Investigation at Buena Vista Lake, Kern County, California," *Smithsonian Inst. Bur. of Ethn. Bull. 180.* Wash., D.C., 1941

WHEAT, Carl I. *The Maps of the California Gold Region, 1848-1857.* San Francisco, 1942

WHIPPLE, Amiel W. "Report of Explorations for a Railway Route, near the Thirty-fifth parallel of Latitude, from the Mississippi to the Pacific Ocean," *Reports of Explorations and Surveys, to Ascertain the Most Practicable and Economical Route for a Railroad from the Mississippi River to the Pacific Ocean . . . 1853-4.* 12 vols. in 13. Wash., D.C., 1855

WILLIAMSON, Robert S. "Report of Explorations in California for Railroad Routes, to Connect with the Routes near the 35th and 32d Parallels of North Latitude," *Reports of Explorations and Surveys, to Ascertain the Most Practicable and Economical Route for a Railroad from the Mississippi River to the Pacific Ocean . . . 1853-4.* 12 vols. in 13. Wash., D.C., 1855

Index

Index

San Gabriel Mountains: 133
San Gabriel River: 113
San Joaquin ("Peticutry") River: 143-50
San Joaquin Valley: 134-35
San José Mission: 146
San Juan Capistrano Mission: 116, 237
San Luis Rey Mission: 118
San Mateo Rancho: 118
San Onofre, Cal: 117-18
San Onofre (Onófrio) Rancho: 117-18
San Pedro, Cal: 125-26, 219, 233
Sánchez, Fr. José Bernardo: 99, 100-02, 105, 108, 126, 131, 149, 216-17, 221-22, 225, 227, 229-30, 232, 235, 239-41
Sandwich Islands: 119
Santa Ana del Chino Rancho: 131, 240
Santa Ana Mountain: 113
Santa Ana Rancho: 113-16
Santa Ana River: 113
Santa Catalina Island: 125
Santa Clara Mission: 146-47
Santa Clara ("Corn Creek") River (Utah): 55, 57-62, 227
Santa Fe, New Mexico: 43
Sardine Canyon (Utah): 41, 197
Sawpit Canyon (Cal.): 93
Schell Creek Mountains (Nev.): 183
Scott ("Scotte"), James (Diego): 107, 124
Screw Mesquite: 72, 76
"Seetskeeder" River: *see* Colorado River
Sevier ("Ashley's") River: 48-50
Shaw, Thomas: 120, 123, 126, 237
Shoshone Mountains (Nev.): 177
Sierra Nevada ("St. Joseph" Mountain): 149-50, 167; attempts to cross, 155-62, 167-70

"Siskadee" (Colorado River) Camp: 66, 210-11
Skull Valley Indian Reservation: 192
Slinkard Creek (Nev.): 172
Smith, Jedediah S: history of manuscript, 11-13; early life in West, 18-20; discovers South Pass, 19; later life, 20-21; personal character, 27-28; commences expedition, 35; members of expedition, 38-39; with Ute Indians, 41-45; in Castle Valley, Utah, 46-47; on Sevier River, 48-51; on Virgin River, 56-66; at Colorado River, 66; at Mohave settlements, 70-85; crosses Mojave Desert, 78-79, 85-91; at San Gabriel, 100-12, 126-30; at San Diego, 119-25; crosses Tehachapi Mountains, 133-34; in San Joaquin Valley, 132-53; crosses Sierra Nevada, 155-62, 167-70; in Nevada, 171-84; in Utah, 184-97; ledger entries, 205, 208, 210-12; in Rogers' narrative, 216-22, 228-29, 232-37, 240-41
Smith, Jackson & Sublette: 20, 35, 39, 42
"Smith's Peak": 161
Snake Indians: 41-44, 54
Snake Mountains (Nev.): 183-84
Snake ("Lewis's") River: 19, 36-37, 176, 192
Soda Lake (Cal.): 88-89
Soda Spring Valley (Nev.): 176-77
Soda Springs, Idaho: 35, 37, 40
Soldier Creek (Utah): 45-46, 50
Soldier Summit, Utah: 45-46, 50
South Pass: 19
Spanish Fork (Utah): 45-46
Stanislaus ("Appelaminy") River: 145, 150, 160, 165-68
Stansbury Mountains (Utah): 189-92, 194

Index